BLACKTHINK

My Life
as Black Man
and White Man

Jesse Owens

with Paul G. Neimark

Blackthink

William Morrow and Company, Inc.

My Life
as Black Man
and White Man

New York 1970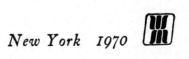

Contents

To a young man
whose color I do not know

BLACKTHINK

My Life
as Black Man
and White Man

1.

I Know the Trouble They've Seen

"Jesse Owens is a
bootlicking Uncle Tom!"
—Harry Edwards, black militant

We'd been driving in our private prison, a dilapidated 1914 Model T Ford, since before dawn. It was almost nine, about our last chance to eat before the track meet in Indianapolis that afternoon.

The rest of the team, the white part, was traveling ahead in five other autos. Shinier ones. It had taken Dave Albritton and me two years to save the $32.50 for the Ford, a minor fortune to a couple of Negroes just a memory away from the nightmare of sharecropping in the South. Dave had worked seven hours a day seven days a week at college to accumulate his $16.25 and I'd held three dif-

ferent jobs six days a week: running an elevator from five
to midnight, working in the school library, and waiting
tables for the white students.

That didn't make us brown Frank Merriwells. Almost
the opposite, in fact. There were thousands of Negroes
who needed those jobs, just as there were thousands of
black men who would have given their right arms—I mean
really given their arms—to go to college. Dave and I had
been able to run a little faster and jump a little better,
so we'd gotten the jobs and the incredible chance to be
the first members of our families to ever go past the beginning of high school, let alone to a genuine place of
higher learning.

There were no athletic scholarships at Ohio State University then, not even if your marks had been good, nor
even if you'd learned how to use your legs to become "the
world's fastest human" the year before. Today, a young
Negro like Harry Edwards can climb out of the ghetto
and go to a tuition-free university, become an articulate
leader, and then use his articulation against those who
taught him the words. Still, if it was nothing compared to
what it took for my father to get out of the South fifty years
ago, Harry Edwards and those like him didn't just leap
out of their poverty and ignorance in one easy vault. You
didn't wish yourself out of the East St. Louis jails where
the Harry Edwardses finally landed because they couldn't
stand drinking drainage ditch water and eating from white
garbage cans, the jails where their brothers and friends
still are. It took grit, the same kind of grit that was at
work when Harry later threw the discus almost two hundred
feet for his school's record.

But when he shouts in one breath that every white man

on earth is no good and in the next tacks up a picture
of me on his wall with the words "Traitor of the Week,"
Harry Edwards is saying that the jails and alleys have
claimed some important part of him—some organ of his
soul, is the only way I can put it. Sure, you can never leave
the past behind, especially not *that* kind of past. You can
never escape scars so ugly and deep they still hurt like open
wounds. But there are some pieces of yourself that you
must keep whole.

I'm no great man. What I've done is no more than
countless other Negroes (and Jews and Poles and Greeks
and just Americans in general) have done. And living fifty-
seven years in this world is no guarantee of wisdom, any
more than a good pair of legs and an exceptional respiratory
system are an automatic ticket to Olympic gold medals.
Even then, it isn't enough to suffer the scars or gain the
brass ring. You've got to find out what's behind them and
tell it like it is, not to the world, but to yourself.

The experience of driving to Indianapolis on that February Friday in 1936 will always be a scar. But now it's a
scar I understand and can take care of. It wasn't that what
happened really hadn't happened before in one way or
another. It had happened a hundred times, maybe a thousand. I lost count long ago. But I do remember riding in
the Ford that day and not being able to keep down the
bitterness that all the Negroes had to be in one car. Not
that it wasn't "natural" in a way. At the university all the
Negroes lived together in one old house. But was *that*
natural?

We'd won a lot of races for our team. I myself had set
four world's records the spring before. We were good enough
to compete alongside the white athletes, but often not good

enough to take showers with them afterward or to ride with them on the way to the meets.

Not that the white fellows weren't a nice bunch of guys for the most part. The majority weren't prejudiced. They were just like almost every other unprejudiced nice guy since the beginning of time, I guess. Their niceness didn't include making sure you got to take your shower, too.

I remember the sun coming out that winter morning and warming my mood for a while. All around us the little farm towns were awakening. Like a kind of giant flower, southern Indiana was opening up. Maybe today it would be open to *us,* too.

Finally the first auto, the one with Coach Larry Snyder driving, stopped beside a roadside eatery. The other cars pulled in behind, and the white fellows began carelessly ambling out in the way athletes move and hurrying in to get their breakfasts. Hungry, we waited in our car until Larry got through talking to the woman behind the counter inside. We watched him out of the corners of our eyes as he leaned toward her, his face growing characteristically red, his hands gesturing to make his point.

When it was over he walked out more slowly than he'd walked in, took a few steps toward our car and simply shook his head. He always bit his upper lip when he had to do this, though it wasn't necessary. We were used to it. We'd never eaten with the white athletes in three years at college, let alone on the road much. At Ohio State, which was one of the more progressive schools, we took our meals in the one ramshackle house where all the Negroes lived. If you were colored and didn't take your meals there, you didn't eat.

Mel Walker and Ralph Metcalfe rifled down the front

window. "What'd they say this time?" Mel called out. It was a rhetorical question, but sometimes you just had to ask it.

Larry took a few steps and shrugged. "About the owner being out and she couldn't take the responsibility."

"Yeah."

We stretched our legs awhile longer on the side of the car away from the restaurant, then got back in and tried to talk track. Ten minutes later a couple of our teammates came out with a stack of thick fresh bread slices and half a dozen plates of big eggs probably from some nearby farm. They were sunny side up, I recall, and the yellows looked like liquid steaming gold as we passed them out among us and started to dig in.

"So this is what they wanted those extra orders for!" shouted a voice next to my window. He was a big man with a paunch. "They told Florence it was for the *other* boys, the ones *inside,* to eat on the road," he yelled, underlining some words like you dug your spikes into the ground to get a foothold before the start of a race. His face was half inside one window of the car, and he was wearing an apron. It was pretty obvious he owned the eatery.

"You were paid, weren't you, mister?" Ralph Metcalfe asked.

"I don't want money to feed no *niggers!*" he bellowed. Then suddenly his arms were inside the car too, jerking at the plates of food. "You give me those!" He lunged, his hands grabbing the plates from us, the silverware and food spilling over our clothes and the seats. Dave wouldn't let go of his and the man flailed out in insane anger, reaching halfway into the auto and hitting down on the plate again and again with his big fist until not a thing was left on it.

Dave dropped the plate then and was out of the car in almost a single motion. I was right behind him, catching him before he got to the man and holding on with all my strength. "No, Dave, no!" I whispered. Somehow I didn't want the man to hear. Dave strained against me for an instant, then dropped his shoulders and just stared into my eyes.

"O.K.," he said bitterly. "What's one more time?"

The man gave a little sneer, not enough to incite Dave again, just enough to tell us he figured he'd won, and walked back into the restaurant with his spoils—six half-empty plates—in his hands.

There were tears in Dave Albritton's eyes when he turned to get back in the car, tears of anger and I think of grief, too. "Now we can eat from the floor," he said, turning away from me. "That's the way it's supposed to be, isn't it?"

For an instant I wavered. For a second or two, just like every other time that it happened, I wanted to let go the way I did when I was running or jumping, really let go, stride into that restaurant and pull that s.o.b. from behind his oh-so-safe little counter and hammer him with all the anger that was in each one of us. But I didn't. I cleared my throat and told Dave that Larry would stop at the next place and get us something. There was still a little time.

"Shit, man, that isn't it," he shot back. "It isn't an empty stomach. It's being empty in *here*." He tapped his chest with his palm. "It's never fighting back. Aren't we ever gonna fight those bastards? Are we always gonna have to call them *mister?*"

"We *are* fighting, buddy," I said. But it came out a whisper like before.

"We are?" he laughed sardonically. He repeated the

words. "Well, then, I've got as much chance of winning as a one-legged hurdler!"

I don't remember what I said after that. I know I wanted to tell him that we were not only fighting, but winning, that the ten million times like this in ten million places didn't begin to add up to the one bigger battle. That was a battle people like the damned restaurant owner didn't even know they were in, and that's why they were going to lose it.

But I knew what Dave would say. The same thing I was saying to myself. *Don't tell it to me. Tell it to HIM.*

Yet weren't we telling it to him when we studied and got our degrees, when we turned the other cheek and went out on the track and distinguished ourselves and gained something to really fight with that no man could take away from us? Or was it the same old carrot they'd been holding in front of our noses for a hundred years?

I believe we beat that man that afternoon. I for one went out there and ran my balls off, ran out all the frustration and anger and fear that was inside me. And afterward, that man from that crumby little restaurant in Indiana walked up to me and did call *me mister*. By asking for my autograph.

Oh, he was changed a little from that morning in front of his diner. His face wasn't so full and he was shorter. Maybe a few years younger, too. But it was the same man, just as it was the same man who came up to me after that and asked me to write my name on his Bible. This time he had his son with him, a nice-looking kid only a few years younger than I was. This time he owned a hardware store that wouldn't sell a nail to a Negro, or worked for a company that only let darkskinned men in the back door for deliveries, or lived in a neighborhood that didn't even allow Negro delivery boys.

And maybe his attitude was different, too. Possibly he wasn't actively prejudiced anymore and beneath it all felt that skin color really didn't make any difference. Beneath it all, that is. Because when everything was said and done he accepted things as they were, and that stood him with the restaurant owner almost as if he'd called me *nigger*.

I feel we beat that man that afternoon, and most other afternoons. But if anyone asks me to say it was a total victory, I can't tell them that. It wasn't. Life doesn't add up that way. And if anyone wants to believe that I've always been absolutely sure, they've come to the wrong place. Harry Edwards is absolutely sure. Rap, Eldridge, Elijah Muhammad—they're absolutely sure.

I've been a Negro in America for fifty-seven years, and I want to tell you it can be pure hell at times and can shake anyone's sureness. Often it's worse if you were the world's fastest human. When you walk into the Pump Room in Chicago or the Plaza in New York wearing a face almost everyone recognizes and still feel that agonizing fear reflex deep in your gut, still can't help wondering with a part of your soul whether the maître d's smile is a sneer and if the woman at the next table thinks you should be waiting on her instead of sitting next to her, it's worse than if you were simply an anonymous black man.

Then there are the nights (and they seem to come more after the good moments because that's when you relax and the fears can really rise to the surface) when you're grabbed from sleep at 3:30 A.M. with the thought you didn't know you even had anymore, but which has actually haunted a secret part of you since childhood.

God, why couldn't I have been born like THEM?

It's an emotion that shakes and demeans you. But most of the time you go back to sleep. When you wake up, it's morning, and you know that the darkness was only daylight's absence. You also know that what you first felt when you walked into a chic metropolitan hotel isn't as important as the fact that the sickly seventh child of a destitute Alabama sharecropper is able to walk into the Pump Room or the Plaza and walk out with the minds of the maître d' and the other guests changed just a little bit about whether black is human.

I don't really care what this headwaiter or that Mrs.-White-Society-at-the-next-table thinks about Jesse Owens. But I have to care what they think about dark skin, because it's right that they should know what's true. It's right because thousands and thousands of kids in ghettos across America deserve the chance to climb out. Every time I or anyone like me can bring the Negro a little closer to them or add a bit of dignity to him in their eyes, those kids have taken a step forward. Oh, it's a small step, that's for sure. It took an awful lot of those steps to make Dave Albritton head of a bank in Ohio and Ralph Metcalfe second man in Chicago politics battling to improve his people's lot thirty-plus years after a nameless white man had pounded their plates of food empty on a dirt road in Indiana.

Those small steps were rough ones too, maybe not unlike the ones Franklin Roosevelt had to take from Campobello, because they never become automatic. You can train your muscles to leap into action within the tenth of a second after hearing a starter's gun, but you can never train your mind to accept hate or the threat of not having the opportunity to earn what you want out of this life. That, you never learn. You always feel like saying to hell with the one-by-one steps, and just get the satisfaction of *now* no matter what direction it takes you in—like the feeling you have when you set eyes on that gleaming new car in the showroom. It's always a temptation to simply get in and drive it away. Except that you know you'll be paying it off for years.

I've driven away a few cars, not all of them economy models. The last time was in the spring of 1968 when I came close to taking one that would have had me paying for the rest of my life, and my children and grandchildren after me. I don't remember yesterday as clearly as I do April 4, 1968.

I was in New York, walking back to my hotel. It was a cool dusk. All at once people began grouping on the streets. I kept walking, but snatches of their talk slowed me. Then I heard it. Martin Luther King, Jr. had been shot. He was dead.

I had to stop and ask the woman who said it to say it again. And then to tell me how she knew. I still wouldn't believe it. The words were like an actual physical blow to me, like running at top speed and suddenly meeting a thick wall of concrete that hadn't been there before.

Martin dead? It couldn't be. Not dead. Hurt, yes. There had always been danger. He had been wounded before.

But *dead*. No. That quiet voice that soothed you and gave you gooseflesh at the same time, that voice that didn't seem to come from his throat at all but from some imperturbable pool miles within him—stilled forever?

I think it was a French poet who said that a great

man's dying is an imitation of the end of the world. Martin's death seemed that to me. In the next hours, the long-buried smell of the Oakville, Alabama, cotton fields—those horrible fifty acres that my father had worked from four-thirty in the morning to eight at night for an almost unknown white man—stifled my senses.

When I got back to my hotel room the phone was ringing. It didn't stop until after midnight. My wife Ruth, from Chicago. My three married daughters. A television station wanting me to participate in a eulogy to him. And then, simply, a lot of people who'd found out I was in New York, assumed I'd known him, and wanted to know what I thought about his death.

I had known him. But what was there to think about his death? Of course, that really wasn't their question. Down deep they were asking what I couldn't stop asking myself: what kind of a world was it where a man like this could be senselessly, brutally taken from us at thirty-eight years of age?

Well, what in the hell kind of a world was it?

One thing I knew. It was a world *I'd* helped make.

That dark Thursday night was a lot like the Friday morning thirty-two years before in front of the diner on the way to Bloomington. Except that now I was thirty-two years older. I'd lived the greatest part of my adult life. *Had* I lived it as a bootlicking Uncle Tom?

I fell asleep about four, but I kept having the same nightmare that jarred me awake again and again. Not of my early childhood in Oakville. Not lying in bed, weakly coughing blood from pneumonia for the third winter in a row because my father couldn't find enough wood to keep the fireplace going. "He's goin' to die! Little J.C. is goin' to die unless we do something, Henry!" I'd heard my mother say to him. Not a nightmare of my later boyhood, either, when we'd moved to Cleveland to find a better life but had found more poverty, if that was possible. No matter how hard my father tried, he couldn't get steady work. There were seven children for my mother to take care of (two had died), but she still hired out as a cleaning woman several hours a day. Even so, there were weeks when we came close to starving. Beans and onions. Potatoes and onions. Bread and onions. And never enough of them. Years passed, and the best my father could do was find a few weeks of temporary work here and there. He never went out on a drunk once during those twelve years, but he did used to sit alone in the corner of the room where most of us slept and just stare at the mottled wall. None of us, not even the youngest, had to be told what he was thinking of doing. Thank God he never did it.

Those nightmares really happened. But the one I had that April night was mostly fantasy and much worse. It left me in an ice-cold sweat, not knowing for a minute whether it was August, 1936, or April, 1968.

I was competing in the Olympics against Luz Long, Hitler's prize broad jumper and, really, against Hitler himself. I was off in a corner of Berlin Stadium, half in the shadows. There were a hundred thousand people there, but none of them seemed to see me. Across the way, maybe about a city block, was the broad jump pit. The jumpers were standing around, jogging in place a little to stay warmed up as the officials called their names. One by one they measured off their steps, raced down the runway, hit the takeoff board and made their marks.

But when was *my* name going to be called?

The shadows were growing longer, and some of the athletes were jumping for the second time. Why haven't they called me, I kept asking myself. But I knew. I knew. The almost inborn fear every Negro must suppress every day of his life, the dread fear that he'll never get a chance to take *his* jump, was rising up from the depths of my mind.

Then it was night. I couldn't see the broad jump pit anymore or the people in the stadium. There was only one face I could make out, and that was because it wasn't a face but a kind of glowing skeleton. It was Hitler. He was leering at me, that same leer I've seen so many times in my life, that half-smile that says people know something you don't know, something about this earth and everyone in it. Something dirty.

I started to curse. It couldn't be. It wasn't that kind of a world, a world where they never called your name and where beautiful young men got shot down in cold blood because they wanted to see every man's name be called. I woke up cursing and sobbing. It was the third time I'd cried in thirty years.

And I only hope that nightmare *was* part fantasy. Because whether you agreed or disagreed with Martin Luther King, Jr., whether you were a black militant or a Wallaceite or any of the fifty things in between, you sensed, even if you tried to hide it from yourself, that this was a genuinely *good* man. You could have seen the films of him with his children in Memphis, you might only have heard him speak a few times, or you may even have had the privilege of knowing him personally.

But you knew it. And it was important, so very important that there was a man like that. I don't get the time to read all that I should, but one of the books I keep going back to is *Walden*. In one place Thoreau says, "It is not so important that many should be good, as that there be some absolute goodness somewhere, for that will leaven the whole lump."

Martin was that absolute goodness. I remember the first time Ruth ever heard him in person. He was speaking at the 49th Street Church near our apartment on Chicago's South Side.

"He's like an . . . *angel*, Jesse," she told me afterward. "He's not a man. He's an *angel*."

I knew what she meant. Yet in the times I spent alone with him, I felt that Martin was very human, more so than the rest of us. I marveled at how he could be so vulnerable and so idealistic, too. Not that there weren't things on which we disagreed. Unlike the simplistic ways of apathy or anger, the way shared by Martin and me is as complex and as full of doubt as man is.

But no one could really disagree with Martin Luther King's soul. After we lost him, and by "we" I mean the world, I wondered if we hadn't been losing all along. It wasn't just that the rational Negro cause no longer had a leader. Even the best of leaders has to be replaced. It was that that absolute goodness had gone out of the world.

And *how* it had been taken away. Brutal, unthinking force had been so effective. Is that the only way to fight back? We spend centuries slaving in manure to grow one man like this, and they snuff him out as if he were a dime-store candle, leaving four children—no, four million children—fatherless.

So I tried those few days in April to come over, Harry Edwards. I needed something, somebody to hate. I wanted to feel there was an easy way out. It was tempting, awfully tempting, to turn my back on my white brothers who so often hadn't been brothers, who had let this happen, maybe made it inevitable.

But not tempting enough. The Negro can never catch his precious quicksilver by making his hand into a fist.

If I had to sum up what I'm going to try and say here, it's that. People have been after me to write this book for quite a while. I've wanted to. A number of times I started putting my notes together. But then I became dissatisfied, felt I needed more time to polish certain thoughts, just as I always used to tell my coaches how I needed "one more practice race before I'm ready."

Life doesn't give you all the practice races you need, though. Not long ago I became very ill, as sick as I'd ever been in the little room in Oakville I shared with my six brothers and sisters. I began *Blackthink* for good after that.

Writing it hasn't stopped me from getting depressed over Martin's death. It hasn't made me any less frustrated when I walk out of the building where we live each morning and look around me. Or when I climb into the car and look into the rear-view mirror—at myself.

But that doesn't mean there aren't some things that should be said, and that aren't being said, things that can show how "the race crisis" going on in America right now is for the most part the biggest hoax in our history. And possibly the cruelest—for in its seeds is another crisis of infinite proportions.

Harry Edwards, my name has never been Tom.

But I *am* old enough to be your uncle.

I know the trouble you've seen. Now can I make *you* —and everyone—see that it's nothing, absolutely nothing, next to the trouble you and your *blackthink* are about to make?

2.

Henry Owens' Tortures

"Suffering? Do you know what suffering is? Suffering is seeing your mother and father sold on the auction block!"

—"The Big Valley"

No one called me nigger until I was seven.

That was because an Alabama sharecropper's child in the First World War years almost never saw the white man who owned his every breath.

Owned.

In theory, the Emancipation Proclamation had been a wonderful thing. But in 1915 in Alabama it was only a theory. The Negro had been set free—free to work eighteen hours a day, free to see all his labor add up to a debt at the year's end, free to be chained to the land he tilled but could never own any more than if he were still a slave.

The blackthinkers of today, often talking from their integrated high-rises, restaurants and universities, don't know what it is to really be shut out like we were then, shut out so tight you actually wondered sometimes if you really existed.

You won't find Oakville, Alabama, on the map today. Eight miles from Decatur, in the northern strip of the state, it was more an invention of the white landowners than a geographical place. Whatever had the smack of civilization to it was in Decatur.

The grocery store was in Oakville, though. Just across the creek. But that wasn't as nice as it sounds. The white man owned the grocery store and he made sure it was awfully convenient. My parents tried not to end up there any more than they had to. Sometimes my father and my older brother Prentis would get up an hour earlier than their usual 4 A.M. to try and shoot a few rabbits for supper. And my mother would find time somehow to tend a little vegetable garden in the back.

But those few rabbits and vegetables didn't go very far with nine mouths to feed. So you always ended up at the owner's store for food, just as you had to go there for tools. My father never paid any money at the grocery. The owner's man just entered our debt on a sheet of paper with #1 at the top—we were the first of eight families who worked his spread of two hundred and fifty acres—and in December of every year, the white man totaled up what you owed against the worth of your crop to find out how much you were ahead.

Only you never came out ahead. It always happened that those "cheap" tools and supplies you bought cost more than the nearly quarter of a million square feet they helped you to plant, just as the weekly potatoes and beans and corn bread (you only bought meat two times a year, on the holidays) always came to more than the six thousand pounds of cotton you enabled the owner to send North.

Each year that it happened, my father went into an angry fit and swore that he was going to learn to read to make sure they were only writing down on that list what he was actually buying. And Mother vowed that she'd learn numbers to check that they weren't charging us too much for it. But there was no one in Oakville to teach those things to them and no time to learn anyway. Besides, my father wouldn't go near a book—he was superstitious about them. That was another holdover from slave days. So one December became the next, and with each one we became a little deeper in debt even though we usually put out more cotton every year than the one before, unless the weevils or some fungus disease had come along.

Our debt was small, though, compared to the other sharecroppers'. We were the "luckiest" family for miles around. My father had been blessed with four sons who had lived. I was the only one who couldn't help, not because I was too young but because I was too sick. Every winter for as long as I could remember, I'd come down with pneumonia. A couple of those years, I was close to never seeing spring.

Yet somehow my mother always pulled me through. Afterward, she'd take my father aside and plead with him to think about leaving the South and sharecropping. He sensed that she was right—every Negro we knew was on a never-ending treadmill of poverty and ignorance—but his fear of the unknown was even greater.

A few Negroes had left and gone North. But Henry

Owens was over forty years old, an age not made by half a dozen Negro sharecroppers in Morgan County. It was late to pull up roots. And like most other sharecroppers, he was the son of the son of a slave. His own grandfather had told him the stories of being *legally* shut out, stories of death that came in the night, sometimes at the hands of the white man and sometimes through simple starvation. So, deep down in that invisible place where a man decides what to do, my father felt that we could have it even worse than we did in Oakville. He wasn't going to dare take a chance on that. The whole world would have to jerk out of orbit for him to pack us up and leave.

And that's just what happened. The whole world, Henry Owens' world, went completely out of orbit.

The first jolt was when I got sick again. This time was different. This time blood came up every time I coughed, and for about a week I didn't know where I was. My mother worked her homemade magic once more, but we all knew it would be the last time. My lungs were too weak.

Our neighbor a mile down was dead. That was the second jolt. My father began sharecropping about the same time Joe had. Joe was a few years younger, and my father had always kind of treated him like a little brother, telling what he knew about better ways to work the land, even lending out one of my brothers to him when things were pretty good, though that wasn't often.

Joe had to work his land alone because his wife kept having stillborn babies. Each time she'd get pregnant they didn't pray for a son but just for something alive. A child would have made life bearable. Yet the years passed and all Joe and Betsy shared were new grave markers in back of their house each twelve months or so.

Then Joe got a "sign." Something told him that Betsy would become pregnant again soon and that this time the baby would not only live but would be a son. When her belly began to swell, Joe's skeleton of a body stopped feeling tired. He worked as never before and whistled every day until the baby came. It came, dead as always. Only this time it took Betsy with it.

So Joe Steppart killed himself.

My father changed after that. Not enough to leave, but enough to begin to think out loud about what that white man and his system were doing to all of us. The white man's name was John Clannon, by the way, and his home was on the top of the one large hill on the other side of the creek. It was too far, of course, for him to see down into our little house. But at night when all the lights were shining on the hill, I imagined I saw him at his big living room window, a window larger than our whole house, watching us.

John Clannon owned two hundred and fifty acres of land with eight men sharecropping it for him. We had the largest spread, fifty acres, because we had the most sons. All the eight houses of the Negroes were on the one side of the creek. John Clannon had never crossed over to that side since he bought the land and carved it up. None of the Negroes ever went on his side, either, unless they were sent for by one of his men.

On a cool night in February of 1921, he sent for my father. We all waited, busying ourselves but not really able to get anything done. "I wonder what the owner can want with Papa," someone would mutter every now and then. What we really meant was, "What was the owner going to do to Papa?" And to us.

For even though we didn't realize it then, we lived

with constant fear. That is the crucial difference between 1920 and, say, 1960. Negroes of a decade or two ago began in poverty and degradation, but the massive machinery of our society was moving to sweep it away. In 1920 there was no machinery. The man on the hill was everything. He was worse in one way than the "benevolent" white despots on slave plantations, because the Negro then wasn't plagued every day by the agonizing choice of what to do with his freedom, whether or not to leave.

In theory, of course, my folks had a fifty-fifty deal with John Clannon, but fifty percent of nothing amounts to nothing. So we lived in fear of him and of his power, and the fear was justified. That February night proved it. My father trudged back into the house almost an hour later and took aside my mother and my older brothers Prentis and Quincy. In our little cardboard house, though, as soon as his voice got agitated it wasn't hard to overhear what he was telling them.

We'd had a particularly good crop that year. Even with exorbitant grocery bills every week, it had still gotten us out of debt. That threatened John Clannon's hold over us, I guess, and he wanted to do something about it right away. What he proposed to do was to revise his deal with my father. Sixty-forty instead of fifty-fifty. Retroactive.

My father had stood still for everything else, but he couldn't stand still for that. The years of resentment had risen up in him and finally become words. He was an un-educated man, but he was a fair man, and he said that this wasn't fair. He didn't get to say it to Clannon himself, though. An "assistant" talked to "the niggers."

"Fair?" the assistant had replied. "What does fair have to do with *you?*" My father was an example, he said. If he could "get the best" of Clannon, the others might think they could too.

"And what about my family?" my father had shot back, finally beginning to lose forty-two years of control. "We work hard. I want my sons to amount to more than I have!"

"Your sons will never amount to anything—just be grateful if they *survive!*" the man had shouted back.

That last statement had stuck in my father's craw. He struggled to spit it out for the next two days, but it only lodged deeper. That Sunday after church he told us that we were leaving Oakville for Cleveland.

We still owed John Clannon some money, but we had our tools and our house and our animals. That would more than pay what we owed and keep us eating in Cleveland long enough, my father figured, for him to find steady work.

My father never found steady work in Cleveland, and we'd had barely enough money to get us North. Clannon offered us next to nothing for everything we owned, including the five mules from Canada my father had scraped and saved for one by one by one. It wasn't just greed that made Clannon do it. He didn't want to let us go. A healthy Negro with three sons who knew the ropes was hard to find.

But we got the hell out. As I said, for my father Cleveland wasn't much different from Oakville. Yet for me it was like another planet. It gave me a chance. And one chance is all you need, no matter what the blackthinkers say.

As I think back, though, I can see part of it was that the white man's words had stuck in my craw, too. *Your sons will never amount to anything.* I wanted to amount to something. I had to. So did a lot of other Negroes whose names you'll never hear, but who *have* amounted to something. That's why when I hear some black militant telling

me and them that we've never made anything of ourselves
and that our sons and daughters never will, I wonder if it
isn't John Clannon's assistant talking again.

It's no accident that the Rap Browns and Stokely Car-
michaels sometimes sound like the Clannons.

Because *blackthink*—pro-Negro, antiwhite bigotry—is
what makes the new Negro and white extremists of today
tick, and it's not much different from John Clannon's *whitethink*. Irrationality and violence, above all, are at blackthink's
gut. It might sound shocking at first, what with all the brain-
washing that goes on, but if you think about it you'll see that
America's blackthinking extremists may be the new George
Wallaces.

Bigotry always begins with a hurt. For the John Clannons it might have been when they got off the boat from
Ireland and found signs that said NO IRISH ALLOWED or ran
into employer after employer who thought that Irish was
another word for *drunk*. Some of those John Clannons
couldn't take it. And their way of copping out wasn't going
on a binge or sailing back to Ireland. What they did was
to work their knuckles to the bone, with bitterness their
twenty-four-hour-a-day boss, and when they got power and
money they took it out on my father and seven other men
and their families. The grandsons of some of *those* families
became the Raps and Harrys of today.

And the hurt was soul-shattering sometimes. It was
rougher than a cancer because, once you had it, you couldn't
cut it out even for a single minute. A couple of years before
we left Alabama I recall hearing about the white mob in
Georgia that lynched a bunch of Negroes because someone
there had murdered the white owner. They never knew if

that someone was a colored man or not. They didn't care. When in doubt about anything, murder a Negro—or a bunch of Negroes—was their creed. Only this time one of the men they hung had a wife who was eight months pregnant and who just couldn't stand to see her husband taken away. She clawed at the shoes of the white men as they dragged him to the tree, she screamed to the next county when they put the rope around his neck.

So they strung her up, too. Only they didn't tighten the knot enough to kill her, just to dangle her above the fire they'd made so she'd slowly burn to death. Before she lost consciousness, her ready-to-be-born baby dropped into the flames.

That wasn't the worst of it. As the baby fell into the fire, the white men ran to their homes to call their wives and their children. To watch it roast.

I feel as sorry for those white children who are alive today as for the dead Negro woman and her child. I shudder to imagine what *their* sons and grandsons have become.

So it isn't that some of today's militants don't have their crosses to bear. And all the atrocities against the Negro didn't happen fifty years ago, either. In World War II a colored soldier could be court-martialed for walking into a white USO, even though the next day he might be shipped overseas to stand in the front line against enemy fire. Of course, not all Negroes were shipped overseas. Two dozen in Alexandria, Louisiana, never got to die for their country. They died for whitethink in 1941 when, for no reason except their blackness, they were lined up and shot in cold blood by some lily-white officers.

The one that somehow sticks in my mind most, though, happened about ten years ago. It was only a squib on the

obituary page of the daily paper. A young Negro artist in
the South had been, without provocation, castrated by three
white men. I think that burned my insides deeper than anything. It seemed to epitomize what so many white men had
really tried to do to the Negro. They hadn't killed him.
Worse. They'd taken away the black man's manhood before
the Negro had ever had the chance to really use it, leaving
an emasculated shell to go through the motions of life for
the next forty or fifty or sixty years. If there is a more sick-
ening crime against the human soul than that, I don't know
what it is.

But I also know that a crime such as this is now the
rare exception. What's more, they are almost always punished, and properly, whenever and wherever they happen.
There *was* a time when horror was a way of life for virtually
every Negro and justice was an impossible dream you didn't
dare torture yourself with. My father only talked about
things once or twice, but that was enough to give me the
picture. Whenever my mother was feeling low, she filled in
the bits and pieces that told you what existence—you couldn't
call it *life*—was like for her parents and grandparents.

Volumes have been written on slave times, from the
near-starvation and the incredible work load that went with
it to the intolerable living conditions and the merciless beat-
ings. We've all heard about the fatherly way the plantation
owners treated some of their slaves, and I'm sure there were
some who did. But my grandparents and great-grandparents
never knew any kindly paternalism. It's said that Alabama
was run by the poor white trash, and that could be part of the
reason. I think the deeper truth, though, is that slave life
was sometimes bearable only for those who, not being able
to live any longer with the never-stopping fright of not

knowing what would happen next, gave in to the tyranny. Like the blackthinkers of today who throw in the towel of reason and angrily lash out as a way of life when they feel they just can't take it anymore, those plantation Toms became allies of the extremists in their day. And let's not kid ourselves—the white slavemasters *were* the extremists, even though they happened to be the Establishment, too. The Nazis were the Establishment in 1936 Germany.

The difference is that today's black extremist is born with a platinum spoon in his mouth compared to what his great-grandparents had to go through. You wonder at times how any one of them then survived mentally, let alone physically. Historian Lura Beam put it better than I can: "The slave lived subject to the fear, shock and pressure that unhinge people now and send them to mental hospitals."

The moments of gratuitous "friendship" from the owners mainly served to underline the basic relationship of master to servant, dictator to subject, human being to lower animal. The whitethinking world my great-grandparents were born into made George Orwell's crimethinking *Nineteen Eighty-Four* seem mild. My own father was actually afraid to *touch* a book! He believed that if he laid a finger on one, someone in the family would fall suddenly ill, possibly die. Primitive? Not altogether. His parents and their parents had never been allowed to own a book, to say nothing of learning to read one. Slaves had been beaten to death for having books hidden in their homes. When we moved up to Cleveland, the first thing my mother saved to buy (and it took almost a year) was a silver-lettered little Bible. She kept it on a special board high above the fireplace and each day every one of us except my father had to take it down and read a passage from it out loud as best we could, any passage, before we left the house. It took my father many years before he could even take the book in his hands. And he never learned how to read it.

Yet if Henry Owens never was able to read the words of his religion, at least he didn't have to dig a hole in the ground or put a kitchen pot over his head to pray. That's what many slaves were forced to do. If they were caught praying openly, they'd be beaten within an inch of their lives, or maybe have their infants—or parents—sold on the auction block as punishment. And if they ever went so far as to try and take their loved ones and run, every white owner had a passel of "nigger hounds" just for the purpose of tracking them down and cornering them like the animals they were felt to be.

So if the white man who owned you "loved" you, it wasn't even in the way that he loved those hounds of his that were always ready to corner you. When a dog died, there might have been a few days of sadness on the plantation. When a slave died, the usual feeling was anger—anger that less work might be done that day. It was up to the other slaves to make up for it, unless *they* wanted to be beaten or starved. Most Negroes didn't have the strength to work any harder, and so they died, frequently before they were thirty, almost always before they were forty. It didn't matter much to the owners, as long as the Negroes kept breeding so a new generation of slaves was constantly growing up to work the cotton. Many of them weren't born with dark brown or black skin, however, because they were the offspring of slave women and the owners. My great-grandfather's wife had to go to the owner's bed whenever "benevolently" beckoned. My own skin isn't light brown by accident or from love, and neither is the skin of any other Negro.

So if Henry Owens was verbally abused, grossly overworked and sadistically treated by the system into which he was thrown, at least he could pray when he wanted and be sure his wife was his alone to love. Leaving this for the North was taking a chance on the unknown, and the unknown could only be worse. That's why it took an earthquake to pry Negroes like us loose from the cotton fields. There was always the possibility of a too terrible past rising up again to haunt us.

I admire my papa fiercely for the decision he made, but you couldn't say it was any more than what his father or grandfather did. Just to survive, in body and spirit, was an accomplishment for *them.*

I've tried to make something of my life, but when I put it against what Henry Owens did, it doesn't seem like much, considering the opportunity I had. And when I put what most of today's blackthinkers, with their opportunities, have accomplished against what Henry Owens accomplished, it comes out near zero.

3.

But Equality Is Here

"If a Negro kid wants to go to college, he can—and usually to the one he wants to go to."
—Chicago Urban League

The tortures of Henry Owens and those who came before are a crucial chapter in the story of blackthink. In fact, any book about the Negro that leaves out the Henry Owenses is being dishonest.

But their story is *only* one chapter.

It is only one chapter because *that torture is over*. The memory may still be painful, it may even be burned into the psyche of many a little colored boy and girl who skip gaily to school today. But, by god, it's *only* a memory. And most of them have a school to skip to.

They have a lot more than that, in fact. Believe it or

not, most black men today start just about equal with the white. We may not begin with as well-off a set of parents, and we may have to fight harder to make that equality work. But we *can* make it work. Because now we have the one all-important gift of *opportunity*.

I know what is usually said. Most whites and Negroes have been brainwashed to believe that black men and women, with a few exceptions such as athletes, entertainers or postmen, don't have much chance in America. It's a lie. If the Negro doesn't succeed in today's America, it is because he has chosen to fail. Yes, there are exceptions. But there are exceptions for whites, too.

I travel a quarter of a million miles a year speaking. One of the things this means for me is countless hours in automobiles listening to the radio and many more in hotel rooms with the television. Radio and TV are mirrors of our culture and all-important means of communication. More obviously than anything else, they show how immensely the race situation has changed. I'm not merely talking about the Negro-generated and Negro-performed music disc jockeys play, or the talk shows that can't get their fill of Negro spokesmen or Negro problems. I'm talking about the people who spin the records and flip the switches and gather the news and run the stations. And *own* them. There are many white-owned radio stations in which Negroes figure prominently, but there also is a mushrooming phenomenon today called *Negro radio*.

I know this from more than listening. I began my own jazz show on radio in the early fifties. It was for a white station. It had to be. After World War II there was only one station in the country even programed for Negroes, let alone owned by them. I played Negro jazz (what else *is* jazz?), but walked the line enough between Basie and Brubeck so that the show couldn't be tagged as Negro. And even then the station worried some.

Today I have the same program—only on a Negro station. No one worries, because there are almost six hundred stations like ours across the country. They are run and worked, sometimes owned, by Negroes. They account for fifty million dollars in advertising annually. The commercials are done by black performers, often through black advertising agencies or through black account executives.

Television tells much the same story. When I'm in a hotel room, I try to write, maybe a speech for the next night, possibly this book. So I don't watch a lot of TV directly, but I often have it on for company. What do I see? Negro detectives and Negro secretaries to white detectives, Negro deans of colleges and Negro confederate soldiers, Negro nurses and Negro doctors, Negroes using aspirin and Negroes buying boats, Negroes—well, you name it. And the chestnut about blacks being big on TV because it's part of the entertainment world just doesn't apply. *These programs reflect our society.* Negro radio and Negroes on TV are only the top thousandth of the iceberg of geometrically growing black economic power and opportunity in America. This year black men and women will spend fifty billion dollars in the United States. *Someone* is doing something besides looting stores or standing outside university administration buildings.

Not that I'm saying these kids who march outside the offices of college presidents are wrong. But I will say one thing: in 1937, it was a different story. Not only didn't a young Negro have time for university sit-ins—he was lucky if he could sit in the classrooms.

I came back from Berlin and the 1936 Olympics to a welcome few people have ever experienced. The streets of New York were lined with tens of thousands of men and women and children wanting to see me—to touch me—as I moved through on the top of a new convertible. It was something else. But it didn't completely fool an Oakville sharecropper's son. Every newspaper had a picture of my face on its front page, and people I'd never met from society and business were buttonholing me to come to their plush suites for drinks and dinners and yachting trips; but one omission stood out more and more as the months passed.

No one had offered me a job.

My mother was taking care of our first daughter back in Cleveland, and now it seemed as though another were on the way. So soon Ruth wouldn't be able to work anymore. It was going to be impossible for me to support a family of four and still get my degree. My brother Sylvester volunteered to help put me through, but I couldn't let him. He was the one who should've gone to college in the first place. He was always the bright one. But like all the others in our family except for me, he didn't even have a chance to finish high school. I couldn't keep taking from them all my life, so I didn't go back to Ohio State University as a senior that fall of 1936. I went to work.

It wasn't as a star halfback for a professional football team, though I think I might have made a good one. Nor was it as a center fielder for a major league baseball team. Negroes hadn't broken into any of that yet. But you *could* say that I went into the general field of athletics and that I capitalized on the ten years of torturous training I'd put my body through.

I became a Cleveland playground instructor for $30 a week.

Fifteen hundred and sixty dollars a year was enough to support a small family, but it wasn't enough to put me back in college. Negroes hadn't offered me anything better because they didn't have anything better to offer, and the white men who wanted me to travel at their expense to their homes all over the country and drink with their sons and chat with their daughters didn't seem to have any openings in their firms except for delivery boys or bathroom attendants.

"What does it pay?" I finally asked one of them.

"Oh, Jesse," he said, putting his plump, pale fingers on my shoulder, "*you* wouldn't want to do something like that after what *you've* had."

So I didn't do something like that. I worked at the playground and came home every night and thought of what I'd had and went off in a corner of our two-room apartment where I hoped Ruth couldn't hear me and put some week-old newspapers in front of my face to try to hide my sadness.

Ruth never said a word. But she knew. It was almost the same for her as it was for me. We'd been childhood sweethearts and had come the long road together. She'd watched me exercise before school every morning until I was slowly molded from a sick, skinny kid into a real athlete and finally into a champion, had walked with me after school to the different jobs I worked. When we did marry at sixteen we'd been able to save only six dollars, and the license, hotel and wedding dinner (a hot dog with all the relish the man would allow) took a lot of that.

But then the good times started to come, the running and jumping records, the headlines, the reporters, the Olym-

pics. My family and I never said it to each other in those
words, Ruth and I never even talked about it, but we were
all thinking: *Can I have broken out? Can a Negro, a poorer-
than-poor colored kid from Alabama, have really broken out?
Was it possible that, even for one black boy, the American
dream was more than a cruel fairy tale?*

My father never would believe it. He didn't want to
spoil the fairy tale for me, but a couple of times he did take
me aside. "J.C.," he confided (James Cleveland was my real
name and he never got used to the new name given me by
people up North), "it don't do a colored man no good to
get himself too high. 'Cause it's a helluva drop back to the
bottom."

And it was.

As the days passed after the Olympics and the best I
could do was make $130 a month watching kids on the
swings, Ruth and I began to feel as though we were being
sucked back into that dark, endless tunnel where every
Negro has to end up.

I couldn't let it happen. I *had* known too much, not
only in the Olympics, but in my dreams. Yet what could
I do about it? I had jumped farther and run faster than any
man ever had before, and it left me with next to nothing.

College was the only answer. If I could just get back
to Ohio State and finish my senior year, something would
come of it. I didn't know how, but I felt that getting a B.A.
would somehow make all the difference. Yet I couldn't return to college while supporting a family of four on my
salary. I had begun to hate my job at the playground as I'd
hated John Clannon. But like my father, I was afraid to
leave.

Then two white promoters came to my apartment one

night. They had an idea, Negro baseball, and they needed a "name" to publicize it. Naturally there were no well-known colored baseball players because none had been allowed in the major leagues, so they had to go outside of baseball. I was a natural choice.

The idea really grabbed me at first. I thought they wanted me to play or at least be manager of one of two teams they planned to have touring the country playing against each other. But that wasn't quite what they had in mind. I wasn't to be connected to the baseball end of it at all. Though, once again, you could say that my athletic prowess would be used.

They wanted me to run a hundred yards against a thoroughbred racehorse before the game each night.

When they said it, I wanted to throw up. They tried to tell me it would be a challenge. I'd beaten every man on earth, now I'd prove I could beat every animal. And I *would* beat the horse, they confided. Because the race would begin with a starter's gun held right near the animal's ear. Before the watching crowd knew it, I would be off to a big lead while the frightened horse was trying to get his bearings. He would cut that lead once he got started but, with my speed and only a hundred yards to run, I'd win by a few inches.

"Nothing doing," I told them in a temper.

"You think about it," one of them said shrewdly. "We'll be back on Sunday."

For five days I swore under my breath at those two white men. For five days I kept telling myself how I hated their idea. But when they returned on Sunday, all the pain of the playground and everything it represented suddenly seemed to well up in me. Before either one of them could get a word out I heard myself say, "I've decided to do it."

So I sold myself into a new kind of slavery. I was no longer a proud man who had won four Olympic gold medals. I was a spectacle, a freak who made his living by competing—dishonestly—against dumb animals. I hated it, hated it worse than working at the playground. But I ran against those horses three times a week, and five cents of every dollar the people paid to watch went into my pocket. It was degrading and humiliating. But it meant that next fall I could go back to college.

Today it's a little different. Like most whites, Negroes who want to go to college do go. And often without having to hold jobs while there or even without a pair of middle-class parents to send them. If "ghetto" high schools haven't properly prepared them, there are hundreds of university-connected programs across the country where they can spend a year boning up before they enter. In fact, not only are Negroes going to college virtually whenever they really want to, but they're going *where* they want.

Of course, that isn't nearly enough today for a lot of black students. It isn't enough for them to attend the finest universities in the world. They want to run them, appoint the teachers, tell the president what courses to have taught. And when they don't get their way, many of them bomb the campuses or burn the libraries.

Why do they do it?

The reasons aren't simple. But one cause is the feeling on the part of many kids, both Negroes and whites, that the new generation is getting a raw deal from society and that the raw deal blacks get symbolizes this. Now I think that even the best university can be improved, and I agree that our society today is far from healthy. But a raw deal?

Are they talking about the more than sixty percent advance in income Negroes have made over the past decade so that the gap between black and white is narrower than ever before? Are they talking about the million new Negro white-collar workers who have sprung up in the last few years? Or the giants of industry who've instituted national campaigns of training, hiring and housing Negro workers at all levels in formerly all-white communities? I travel 100,000 miles a year for Ford Motor Company alone, and I know that the executives in the big companies across this country today really do want young Negroes, just as I knew that they *didn't* want *me* in 1937.

Look around you. Look deep, and believe what your unlying eyes tell you, not what the fire-fanning blackthinkers hand out.

Did there used to be discrimination in the army? Well, in the last four years the number of Negroes on draft boards has increased three hundred percent. There are dozens of black colonels and even black generals—one of them a woman.

Did the Ku Klux Klan used to have power in the South? Right now most Klan leaders are in jail or on their way there. Those who aren't are running scared, just as the Negro used to run.

Yes, things have changed—drastically. In fact, if we're going to tell it true, things have sometimes gone too far and turned completely around. Because for every anti-Negro bigot—and there're still too many—it seems as though there are two pro-Negro bigots today.

The man sitting next to me on the plane was middle-aged, obviously successful and white. He didn't recognize my face, he only recognized me as a Negro. He waited for what he thought was the right moment to begin the same conversation with me that hundreds of white people have.

First there were the amenities. Not good weather for the flight, was it? Would I rather have the seat near the window—he didn't mind. Had I seen the movie?

All very innocent, if a bit too solicitous. But who can knock friendliness? And sometimes it *is* friendliness. Sometimes this kind of small talk isn't just a bridge to what they really want to talk about, race, and *why* they want to talk about it—to show they like me, even though they've never seen me before in their lives.

"Speaking of that, how do you think Nixon's 'black capitalism' is working out?" he asked at the first possible connection, no matter how remote.

"There's capitalism and then there's *capitalism*. Is that a Boston accent I detect?" I answered, trying to change the subject.

"Yes. Well, I think it's going to work," he went on. "Your people are really going to benefit."

I tried another time. And then one more. I didn't mind talking to him, didn't mind talking to him about race, but not this way.

"Look," I finally said when I could see it was no use. "How many Negroes do you *really* know?"

He retreated defensively. "Well!" he blurted, "I was just trying to be friendly—and *polite!*"

Politeness is a virtue. And real friendliness is all too rare in our busy world. But this man was neither. He was being overly gracious to me, one of the most obvious forms of *re-*

verse bigotry. He simply wouldn't see me as anything else but a Negro. I wasn't a fellow passenger on a flight encountering some bad weather, or a man who might or might not want to see the movie or prefer the inside seat. I was a *thing* wrapped in brown skin.

One of my friends in Chicago is a psychiatrist. White. Wherever he goes socially, whether it's a cocktail party or a poker game, people hardly ever let him forget his work. "Oops—that was a Freudian slip, wasn't it?" Or, "But I guess that's just one of my fantasies!" It hardly ever stops. He happens to be a very dedicated doctor who loves his work. But he's also a whole man, with all of the desires and interests and activities and problems of a whole man. Most of all, he goes to cocktail parties or plays poker with the boys to forget the couch and the problems of those on it.

Negroes are *people*. Many of them, most of them, are vitally interested in the race problem. They spend a good deal of their time trying to deal with it or things relating to it. But they eat and sleep and work and love and play and worry, too. And if they don't do these things, they won't be any damned good with the race crisis or any other crisis in this world.

Yet reverse bigotry is all around us today. In most intellectual circles and many middle-class ones, black is "in." What one writer called "the black gold rush" is on. "Instant Negroes" has become a familiar term in business and education. The treasury department threatens to withdraw its money from banks that haven't hired Negroes, but where are they going to get Negro bankers? Extremists demand that Negro history be taught only by black teachers. *What* black teachers?

But if there aren't enough teachers or bankers yet,

there're enough men and women and children simply
wrapped in brown to produce *reverse social discrimination*
in most strata of our society. "Have you had your Negro for
the week?" is a line in the act of one night club comic I know.
Or: "You bring the punch, Alice; you bring the extra card
tables, Barbara; you bring the canapés, Cheryl; and I'll bring
the Negroes."

One particular bit of humor tells it best of all, though.
The young Negro mother had just moved into the white
neighborhood, to the feverish enthusiasm of every white
woman. They were gathered around her, chattering com-
pliments and invitations.

"Now Monday you'll come with me to the PTA. We want
you on the Steering Committee," one said.

"Tuesday afternoon you'll go shopping with me and
that night there'll be bridge at the Talbots'," the next said.

"Wednesday is Women's League and Thursday is the
neighborhood coffee klatch," another put in. "And Friday
is theater," the fourth said. "You *must* sit in our box."

"And Saturday," still another woman added, "you'll have
to see the new art exhibit with Phil and me."

A bewildered look settled on the young Negro woman's
face. "And what about Sunday?" she asked.

"Oh," said the white women in chorus, "Sunday you'll
have off!"

The deep, disturbing truth in this jest is that bigotry in
reverse is still bigotry, still stems from the same myth of
Negro inferiority, and still ends up making the black man
or woman a thing or an issue or a project or a problem at the
expense of not making him or her a *person*.

Of course, it would be astounding if discrimination in
reverse didn't exist today. The imbalance of centuries can't

be restored without the pendulum sometimes swinging too far in the other direction. But at the same time it's important to recognize reverse bigotry for what it is, and to know how it works hand in hand with blackthink. It is important to know because reverse bigotry stems partly from white guilt and fear, and actions taken out of guilt and fear end in resentment and violence. It's also important to know the nature of reverse bigotry, because of the bad feeling it spawns in the Negro. Bigotry against us because of our skins is sick, but at least it is out-and-out sickness that every reasonable person condemns. Bigotry *for* us because of our skins is an insidious emotional tokenism that can quietly widen the breach between black and white, liberal and moderate, young and not so young.

Still, reverse bigotry is dwarfed by the true catastrophe of today—that the Negro is in danger of being maliciously, tragically brainwashed.

4.

Negroes Have
Human Hangups

"American Teachers Association
m: 37,000
to provide equal educational
opportunities for all children
and equality of professional
status for all teachers.

Alpha Kappa Alpha Sorority
m: 40,000
to encourage high scholastic
and ethical standards, promote
unity among college women
and to be of service to mankind.

Ancient Egyptian Arabic Order
Nobles of the Mystic Shrine
m: 24,000
to enhance the work and programs of Prince Hall Masonry,
promoting local and national
charitable, civic, educational
and economic development
programs.

Alpha Kappa Mu Honor Society
m: 6,680
encourage high scholarship
among college undergraduates
and scholarly achievement
among the alumni.

Ancient and Accepted Scottish
Rite Masons
m: 20,000
dedicated its program to fraternal and charitable causes,
with emphasis on civic and
educational activities.

Alpha Phi Alpha Fraternity
m: 8,000
to develop a strong unit of college trained men dedicated to
social uplift and progress
through eduation, active citizenship and the creation of a
climate of good-will."

—Entries under "A," Negro Organizations,
The American Negro, by Irving J. Sloan

Pete is a Negro who talks with a smile, and always reason-
ably. He's so reasonable, in fact, that both Negro and white
friends have called him "the one black man who's been left
untouched by prejudice."

A forty-three-year-old college graduate with an excellent
job on a large metropolitan magazine, Pete smiles when
people tell him how "amazing" his lack of anger is. But inside he seethes. For inside is a staggering mountain of hostility, and, every few months, it boils over and Pete's attractive wife goes to her job wearing too much makeup,
which doesn't quite hide the bruises on her face.

Or Pete simply disappears. He waves goodbye to the
secretaries and his fellow writers Friday afternoon (after
covering stories all week with a talent that has won him the
admiration of every editor in the city), gets into his 1969
Buick and isn't seen again until Monday morning. Sometimes he stumbles into his apartment Sunday night looking
like he's been on Skid Row the last five years. Sometimes his
wife Corinne gets a call Sunday afternoon, hears his voice
at the other end of the wire in some small town fifty, maybe
a hundred miles away, no longer drunk but now drained of
all emotion, whispering, "Come and get me . . . will you,
honey? I'm in no shape to drive. . . ."

Corinne takes the name of the hotel and the town from
her husband, hangs up, dries her eyes, leaves a note for their
fourteen-year-old, who is out practicing with his rock-and-
roll group, and calls a cab. Monday morning Pete will be at
work bright and early, his smart sport coat and just-conserva-
tive-enough tie catching the eye of almost everyone around
him. He'll sit down at his typewriter and begin banging out
a lead on a story, and at the desk next to him or in the secre-
tarial pool across the way or even behind his boss's glassed-in

office, someone will be thinking, "Now there's a colored guy who doesn't know he's colored."

And they're right.

Pete is angry. Pete is violent inside. Maybe even sick. But not because he's a Negro. Because he's a man—with a man's problems. Pete and Corinne, you see, have never, not once in fifteen years of marriage, been really able to make it in bed together. And it's destroying them both.

The clock-radio wakes me at a little past seven when I'm at home. Some sweet music lifts me out of sleep, soon followed by the voice of Eddie Morrison or Joe Cobb, Negro disc jockeys who got up earlier than I did to do their thing.

Ruth makes me breakfast while I dress, just as hundreds of thousands of Negro women are making breakfast for their husbands all over the city of Chicago, and in thousands of other places across the United States. By a quarter to eight I'm in the elevator on my way to the car. Our elevator is automatically operated, but in the city of Chicago there are countless buildings with operators to run them, and engineers who designed them, and maintenance superintendents to take care of them. Many of them are Negro, just as the doctors and delivery boys, businessmen and burglars who ride in them are often Negro.

The lobby is fairly crowded as I walk through. The building is twenty-seven floors high and a lot of husbands are going to work. I see one I know in Brooks Brothers gray and nod. I see another in an iridescent steel-blue and nod again. The first has dark skin, the second white. Otherwise, it's hard to tell the difference. They're both successful lawyers.

Traffic is bad and, as I approach the Loop, I'm driving

in stops and starts. I switch off the radio to save the battery
and look around me at the men in the other automobiles.
Some are scowling, some are smiling. One seems to be singing. Another is trying to read his newspaper, still another is
eating a sweet roll and drinking what must be coffee from a
thermos. A teen-age couple are cuddling.

Some are white, some are black. Some are yellow. The
fellow with the thermos may even be an Indian—his cheek-
bones are high, and he has an unusual ruddiness to his face
that sunlamps don't give.

Does it matter?

Of course it doesn't. Just as it doesn't matter whether
this particular parking lot attendant or that specific secretary
at my first appointment is Negro or white. In the next twelve
hours, I'll talk to dozens of people, laborers and waitresses,
policemen and parking lot attendants, salesmen and scholars,
bartenders and beggars. Yes, there will be more white than
Negro executives, and the shoeshine boys are still all Negro.
But the deeper point is that these are the majority of Negroes
in the average American city, these and their unseen wives
and husbands and children, going about *their* business, doing
their thing.

And they are not merely "the majority." They are the
overwhelming majority.

Pete is one of them. And I doubt that even the wildest
eyed black militant or the most far out white liberal will try
and tell you (much as they'd like to) that the root of Pete's
problem is his skin color, that his impotency comes from the
supposed psychological emasculation of the Negro male by
the white race. Because part and parcel of that emasculation
myth is the phony legend of Negro sexual superiority. The
black man, the story goes, made up for his suppression in

the only place that he could: bed. He has thus come to be a supreme sexual animal, a tireless and incomparable lover.

That, of course, is crap. Some white women may respond more to Negro men because black lovers are taboo, and Negro men generally may be more culturally uninhibited than WASPS and Jews and Britons (though less than Italians and Frenchmen and Berkeley students), but that doesn't change the Negro into Superlover. Every black man when he gets into bed with a woman has the same problems that *men* have, tempered by his own individual personality and values.

Like Pete.

Pete had what is known today as a "Jewish mother." She's pretty prevalent among Negroes, too. And among most other families. A hundred years ago it might have been different. But today a whole new generation of Negro males has grown up who were raised in middle-class homes by a mother who sometimes doted on the first son to the point where he couldn't cut it later in a mature male-female relationship. I realize that this also contradicts the phony myth of the typical Negro family as hopelessly fragmented, with the mother either an unwed welfaree or "widow" to a man who has left her long ago.

Of course, Pete's problem wasn't as simple as a dominating mother. He had other hangups. But none of them were connected to the color of his skin. If someone told you all about them without telling you he was colored, you'd assume he was an "average" American white—if there is such a thing.

Pete started worrying about his masculinity in his early teen years. At the same time he started rebelling against his mother. He didn't want her to control him, but he secretly felt lost without her. That was always the way it was with him. He strove to make a man of himself, became a two-letter athlete in college, got his degree with honors and went on to distinguish himself in the navy and then in his chosen career, but always was torn inside by the feelings his child-hood had wedged into him.

Marrying Corinne was his biggest attempt to break with his past. She wasn't anything like his mother. Corinne was intelligent, attractive and thoroughly feminine. Maybe too much so. She would've been a real challenge to a normal man. To Pete, her mature femaleness was almost a reproach, and it paralyzed him sexually from the beginning.

Corinne tried to help him, he tried to help himself. But it was too late for Pete to be able to cure his mind by using that same mind. He needed a psychiatrist and was too proud to see one. "Hell," he said to me once, "if I can make it to the top at an all-white university, on the hills of Korea and in this publishing jungle, I ought to be able to make it where every junkie and bum in the city does. In bed."

The weeknights were the worst. He could no longer face Corinne in the bedroom. So he'd stay in the kitchen drinking and fall into bed at one or two in the morning after she was asleep. Only she wasn't asleep. Corinne knew Pete had problems when she married him, but she thought he'd grow out of them. Even when she found that those neuroses were deeper than they looked, discovered that the passionate petting sessions they'd had wouldn't turn into a full man-woman relationship—they were both virgins at marriage—she felt that they'd still work it out.

She didn't let Pete escape. Their son was becoming more aware as the years passed, and this made it harder, too. So Pete eventually began not coming home at all on the weekends and "working late" on weeknights at a bar near his home.

Pete has everything to live for and he knows it. He's intelligent, educated, makes good money and, like a geometrically increasing number of Negroes, has never really been bothered emotionally, socially or professionally by the color of his skin. He had an incident or two in the navy and several at college before that. And it wasn't that he didn't hear the word *nigger* as a kid, either. But no one ever put a chain on his ankle or told him that survival was all he could ask for. And if being called a name or two is enough to throw you permanently out of orbit, then every Jewish and Italian and Irish and Polish person—to say nothing of white Anglo-Saxon Protestants, who are currently as "out" as *out* can be—would be a mental case.

No, Pete has it all, but, tragically, he doesn't have the emotional tools to make it work for him. So inside he's a pressure cooker of hate and anger and violence. And none of it, not one single part, has a damned thing to do with the race problem.

J. has his problems, too. He's another typical Negro today, a black man who doesn't have it easy in this world, but not because of his blackness.

J. was born in the same year I was. He had to leave school at thirteen, got a job as a janitor in an apartment building in Detroit and married early. His wife Grace worked hard too, and, even with the Depression, they were able to save so that by the early forties they'd put away enough money for a down payment on a modest home. Grace bore two sons seven years apart, and the J.'s lived a quiet, relatively happy life.

What I mean by *relatively* is that they were *happy*. But

they did have much the same problems every married couple has. There were periods when they fought, and more than once J. stormed out of the house. J.'s job gave him fits now and then too. He was no longer the janitor of one small building but the "maintenance supervisor" of it and a dozen houses as the man he worked for—Negro, by the way—became more successful. Finally, J. had a staff of several people who janitored for *him,* while he took care of the larger responsibilities. Before he knew it, he was running a small work force for his employer, with problems that began as soon as someone didn't show up at 6 A.M. and didn't end until some furnace stopped acting up at five the next morning.

J. didn't like the problems, but for a man who only went through eighth grade and whose parents had been poor southern laborers, he was kind of proud of himself, too. Yet he had always had a dream: to send his sons to college. He couldn't do that on $155 a week. "If I can run someone else's business—and that's what it amounts to—why can't I run my own?" he asked his wife. "A business of our own could mean $155 a day sometimes!"

"And nothing other times," his wife told him. They then got into one of the biggest arguments they'd ever had, with Grace going all the way home to South Carolina for an entire week. But she returned—and they patched it up as always

J. wears glasses, has gray hair and walks with a shuffle. He looks like a studious, meek man, the kind of man you might expect to be a college professor if his skin were white. But he isn't meek. In the spring of 1957, he sold his house, quit his job and began a cleaning shop in a plush, nearly all-white Detroit suburb. Of course, when you say nearly all-white, you are saying that four, maybe eight percent of the people living there are black. Since the percentage of

Negroes in the overall American population is only twelve percent, that really isn't staggeringly low. It isn't nearly as high as the "ghetto," but it adds up to a new and significant segment of Negroes across the country. In this particular suburb, it meant fourteen hundred people out of thirty-seven thousand.

J. was the only Negro who owned a business there, though. You might think that fourteen hundred Negroes bringing their cleaning to him would have assured him success. As a matter of fact, fourteen hundred regular customers would have made him a pretty wealthy man. But those other Negroes didn't race to J.'s Cleaners. Most of them went to one of the other five cleaners in the area, because the shops were closer, or advertised more, or gave stamps.

J.'s Cleaners was more convenient to many homes, though, and he started advertising, too. With Grace working in the store, the J.'s acquired a steady group of customers and began making money. In the beginning, it wasn't $155 a month, let alone in a day, but the money from the house they'd sold saw them through, and within a couple of years the store was prospering. In 1961, the J.'s moved from an apartment back into a house, a nicer home than they'd had in Detroit, and in 1964 their first son entered college.

But as I said, J. has problems. Now he's responsible for twice as many people as he was in Detroit, some of them white people. He and Grace can still get into some pretty mean arguments. Yet let's face it—those aren't problems. What *is* a problem is J.'s younger son. J. has worked hard all his life for one goal above all: to put his sons through college so that they could be more from the start—a lot more—than janitors. And now his younger boy doesn't give a damn. He not only doesn't care to go to a university when he graduates from high school next year, but he won't be able to if he changes his mind. His marks are terrible, and he'll be lucky just to get his twelfth-grade certificate.

The brainwashers of blackthink will make just one more damning statistic out of him, though: another poor Negro kid who couldn't make it into college. The truth is that Skip may not make it into a lot of places. He's been arrested twice for shoplifting and once for being caught at a wild pot party. There've been a number of other incidents, too, because half the time the boy is whacked out on marijuana. It's only because J.'s an upstanding member of the community that his son isn't in jail right now.

I'm not completely condemning young J. Though a lot of rigid phonies from my generation wouldn't agree, he has his problems too. Big problems. But he's still breaking his father's heart. I realize that's a cliché. Yet J.'s problem with his son is almost a cliché today. It has nothing to do with being black.

Not all Negroes have such troubles. Richie, for example, is concerned with "problems," but doesn't really have any.

Richie is twenty-four years old and definitely a member of the younger generation. He graduated from a West Coast college two and a half years ago, and while he was in college he smoked pot, demonstrated, grew a beard and all the rest.

But about the only thing left now is the beard. Not that Richie doesn't go to rock-and-roll bars and doesn't distrust a little anyone over thirty. But he's also come to distrust some of those under thirty he used to demonstrate with, the ones who couldn't cut the cord from college, who are still around there at twenty-four, twenty-six and older, not really to study, but to instigate.

Not that Richie has thrown in with the Establishment. He got fed up with the rat race in college and, if he didn't want to become a "predator" like a few of his revolutionary friends, he didn't want to become a victim either. So Richie became a mailman.

I'm not implying that there's anything wrong with being a mail carrier. It's simply that college graduates with a 91.2 average usually go into a profession. Richie's parents had always wanted him to be a lawyer, and he certainly has a talent for words and logic. But he couldn't see spending his life arguing the kind of things lawyers usually spend most of their lives arguing today. Richie was interested in more than whether a zoning line was in the middle of someone's property or whether a corporation could save a few thousand dollars by merging with a firm in another state.

He thought of becoming a teacher. There he could confront what he felt were the important things, whether in philosophy or world affairs. But four years in college "cured" him, Richie said. He felt his professors were "out of touch." He had come to feel that just about everyone was, in fact. And the only answer seemed to be to stop pretending everything was so almighty important, to stop being involved. So Richie, former Phi Beta Kappa and student demonstrator, dropped out in his own way.

He didn't become a hippie or a hermit, but he did decide to free himself completely from the pressures of the world. He joined the National Guard, doing his army stint mainly by going to camp for a few weeks every summer.

He looks on it as a kind of vacation. Richie hasn't even had a cold since 1968, so he's also able to take his post office sick time skiing in Colorado or surfing on the beach in California.

Two hundred and some odd days a year, though, he delivers mail. He makes it a kind of challenge (like it used to be to see how fast he could master Kant or Aristotle) to try and get his whole route done in the mornings. Usually he does. What he'll do then is to stop off at the local YMCA. Richie walks in, smiles at everybody in a kind of knowing way (as if to say, "I've broken the back of it, buddy, why haven't you?"), casually peels the orange he always has with him and reads the morning paper for about twenty minutes. Then he goes to his locker, suits up and plays an hour or two of handball. He's one of the Y's two or three best players.

Afterward, he takes a shower and lounges around in the TV room with a towel around him, eating a late lunch that he packed for himself the night before. People have said Richie looks like a cat when he stretches out on the short couch there, his head on the hardwood table, so at ease in his healthy, animal-like way. Sometimes he dozes for awhile, then leisurely dresses and reports back in to the post office. At night he may date one of several girls or have a couple of fellows over to his apartment for cards or just sit alone and read or watch a little TV.

Richie keeps up with world affairs—he's more conversant with most issues than almost anyone I know—but he stays thoroughly detached from them. The same knowing grin he greets you with is there even more when he reads how politicians and people in general often make a mockery of things. He and one girl felt pretty attached to each other last year, but didn't get all the way to marriage. "I guess we just didn't feel quite strongly enough," he told me when I passed an afternoon at his Y while speaking in California not long ago.

It would be a temptation to say, "What a waste," when talking about Richie. But I'm not absolutely sure his life is such a waste. When he looks around him, especially at his three older brothers, *he* certainly has no doubts. All are professional men, one in the process of losing his wife and four children through a grisly divorce, the second going to a psychiatrist three times a week, the third suffering from ulcers and migraine headaches.

"That's success?" Richie once asked me.

Anyway, I'm not psychoanalyzing Richie. I'm here to point him out and to say that there are many like him, so many that they form an important new part of the Negro middle class—and the American middle class—a lot more important part that the shouting militants. Richie, former demonstrator, former anarchist, former professional black man, now lives a quiet, contented life three hundred and sixty-five days a year, a life that maybe is too quiet, but which has nothing, absolutely nothing to do with the color of his skin.

Pete, J., Richie. They aren't Sidney Poitier (though he has his problems, too, believe me). But what they *are* is the new American Negro, outnumbering the extremists by a hundred, maybe five hundred, to one.

Not that the new Negro isn't usually deeply disturbed about things in our society—Vietnam, nuclear war, violence in the streets, the generation gap, inflation *and* the race problem—just as most white citizens are. Exclusively Negro organizations dedicated to dealing with these problems, organizations like the American Teachers Association, the National Association for the Advancement of Colored People, the National Bankers Association, the Association for the Study of Negro Life and History, the National Conference of Artists, the National Newspaper Publishers Association, the National Medical Association and so many, many others, are proof. Just about any one of these groups has more members than all the different kinds of militants put together.

Of course these organizations and the people in them never get the headlines. Like a Jonas Salk or a George Washington Carver, they work in their "laboratory" unknown and unpublicized, until they finally come up with something so startling that the world has to stand up and take notice. But when their laboratory *is* the world, the project never shows any sudden or spectacular results.

These blacks, fifteen million strong of them, are where it's really at with the Negro people. The Richies and J.'s and Petes and their families are the *silent black majority* that has neither spoken nor been spoken for.

I'm one of them. I've always been one. And I'll tell you two things about us. First, we don't always agree with one another on what should be done about Vietnam, nuclear war, violence in the streets and all the rest. In fact, I am often as opposed to what our leading "moderates" have said as I'm against the rantings of Rap Brown, Jim Forman or Harry Edwards. But, second, not one of us, not a one, would any more riot, any more think of revolution, than we'd board a boat back to Africa because of what was done to our great-grandfathers.

I know, because what's true of Pete, J. and Richie is true of Jesse Owens. I knew the bitterness of not being able to earn more than $30 a week as a playground instructor after I'd become one of the most famous people on the globe, of being segregated from white athletes after I'd broken world's records they'd never attain. I knew the terror of sharecropping in the South.

But I've lived with and worked with whites as if I were one of them and still had it rough—just as a man. My life as black man and white man have both been struggles.

When I finally went back to college, for instance, I thought my troubles were over. But the same personal weakness that had allowed me to sell myself out and run against frightened racehorses wasn't educated away by a few courses in history or English. Just before I graduated, a man came to me with a proposition. Did I want to make a million dollars on my name without ever lifting a finger?

Running against the horses had been a bad experience for me in another way. I had made thousands of dollars for doing what I used to do for nothing and without any real fear of losing. So I believed this guy. Sure, I said, I'd like to.

I met with a couple of other men, signed some papers and, before I knew it, cleaning stores bearing my name were springing up all around Cleveland and in other towns, too. And they boomed. Or so it seemed. Whenever you walked into one, there was a line. Most of all, whenever I asked my partners how we were doing, they'd answer by handing me money. That was in addition to my hefty weekly draw. I'm not talking about lunch money, either. The checks were in four figures a lot of the time.

Ruth told me I should ask to see the books. "Why?" I asked. "Nobody gives away money for kicks. They must be running the business right. One of these days I'll have a lawyer take a real good look. But I just can't right now. They're being too good to me. It's better than running against racehorses."

And it was. For a while. I didn't have to work more than an hour a day. If I wanted to speak somewhere, I could do it without worrying about the fee. Ruth and I went on trips. Most important of all, I was able to buy for my mother and father a fifteen-room house in Cleveland.

But they didn't live in it long. The house had to be sold in 1939. Because one day in the fall of that year, I couldn't get hold of my principal partner. I tried to reach the other ones. "They're out of town," I was told.

I needed money. I'd been spending it like the world's fastest human. Oh, we'd saved a few thousand, but tax time was creeping up again, and I'd planned to buy something special for Ruth and Gloria that Christmas. Gloria was turning into a first-class cook just like her mother even though she was only going on eight, and the kitchen had become an important room of our own house. I'd had a completely new one with all the latest appliances built in miniature and was going to put that model under our tree.

We never did get the kitchen and I never reached my partner. Instead I was served with a subpoena. Our corporation, for which I was suddenly solely responsible, was bankrupt. Creditors were suing us for debts we had never paid. I had to come up with the money within thirty days or every Jesse Owens Cleaning Store would be boarded up and the equipment sold at auction.

That was the first I ever heard of any debts or anyone suing us, and I couldn't have paid if I'd run against horses a dozen times an hour seven days a week. So the stores were boarded up, an auction was held and the equipment sold. Ruth and I put our house on the market and, with Gloria and little two-year-old Beverly, moved in with my parents. Three months later they gave up their home and went to a cheap apartment. In front of that house was left the oak tree I had been awarded for setting a record that would last twenty-four years in the Olympic broad jump. I only wondered how long my debt would last.

It turned out to be five years, and they were grotesque. Now I knew how my father felt. Worse. For as his eyes had predicted to me, I *had* come down to the bottom after falling all the way from the top. For fifty-nine months, I once again held three jobs, my family living close to the bone, so that dollar by dollar we could save to make up that $55,000 I owed.

It meant seeing my third baby, Marlene, born into the poverty I thought had been left behind for good. It meant uprooting ourselves—leaving my parents, brothers and sisters—and moving to Detroit, because that was where the best job offer was, hiring all wartime Negro personnel for Ford Motor Company. I hired almost fifty thousand Negroes during those years.

It also meant that I couldn't serve my country actively in World War II. I'm not gung ho on wars, and I think any youngster who doesn't want to go off to Vietnam has a point. Fighting the Nazis was different, though.

But I had to pay off my debt. I just couldn't declare bankruptcy, and so the government had me work in one of the biggest war plants. When I was through at five, I'd head across town to teach some youth groups, and on weekends I'd speak. About the same time that Patton's tanks crunched through France on the way to Berlin, I paid off the last penny I owed.

Those years were hell. Both my parents had taken sick and died. I was watching my daughters grow up (Gloria was nearly a woman) without being able to give them the things that the factory people under me gave their kids. I watched Ruth, who had come such a long way with me and deserved better, darning ragged hand-me-downs just as my mother had in Oakville twenty-five years before. And when I saw my mother every few months back in Cleveland before she passed away in 1940, I couldn't escape the pain in her eyes, the pain of seeing the world collapsing as my father had always known it would—of seeing the one son of hers she thought could break out reduced to spending his life paying off debts some unknown white men had put on him.

But let's be honest. What I went through was nothing compared to what happened to a lot of other Americans from 1941 through 1945. And, what's more, I deserved what happened to me. I deserved every grim guilt that threatened to hunchback my soul. I had been stupid, the kind of stupid that no college can ever cure. I had forgotten what it took to become the world's fastest human, the incredible sweat and pain and years. I had begun to believe what the newspapermen were writing about me, that fate had thrown me up against Hitler and that I was destined to shame him.

And so I shamed myself. I started, little by little, to believe in the easy way. The devil that sits on all our shoulders every day of our lives got deep inside me. That may sound dramatic, but that's the way it is, and I think we all know it.

So, those five years taught me that there *is no easy way*. The militants and ultraliberals who want it all served up quick and neat are whistling "Dixie." And I mean literally, because they're no different from the Dixiecrats of another day who wanted to go back to a primitive world that mostly never existed, and that never should have been allowed to anyway.

But if all this is true and at bottom the "Negro problem" is only one more human problem, how do Pete, J. and Richie jibe with the myth of the Negro as either ghetto derelict or angry extremist?

They don't.

It's the Harry Edwardses who have sold themselves (and are threatening to sell America) on this myth, just as some southern landowners sold us another myth a hundred and fifty years ago.

How can a small group of writers and political activists have such a staggering influence? That's what's so dangerous about blackthink and why it's so important to expose it. A midget can paralyze a giant by putting one finger in the right spot on his neck. The course of history has often been guided by the few who knew its pressure points. The chances are much less of this happening in a free country, but it's still possible.

The sad fact is that a hypersensitive and naïve public, an often out-of-touch "moderate" leadership and a sometimes headline-hungry press have played perfectly into the hands of the blackthinkers. The last Olympics were an example. What will be remembered by the American public? Bob Beamon's incredible twenty-nine-foot leap in the broad jump? Randy Matson's breaking the Olympic record in his first shotput try? Al Oerter's fourth straight gold medal in the discus (when he worked in an aircraft factory and could practice only forty-five minutes a day)? Billy Toomey's decathlon record? Wyomia Tyus's great hundred-meter triumph? No, the 1968 Olympics will always be remembered here for the Smith-Carlos incident, where two black runners from the U.S. gave a black-power salute on the victory platform and were sent home by the Olympic Committee.

Big deal.

I've seen whole countries pull out of the Olympics. And there have been athletes sent home for misconduct every year since the Games were formed, and that goes back to ancient Greece. Whenever you get thousands of young men together, you're bound to have a few that will become too rowdy. But this wasn't merely a case of rowdyism. This supposedly had tremendous overtones for all the American athletes and for the race problem itself.

Believe me, the Smith-Carlos incident had as many overtones in Mexico City as two grammar school kids trying to create a tidal wave by skipping stones in the Pacific Ocean. I know what *Life* magazine said. I know what virtually every newspaper in the United States said. And I also know the truth—because I was there, not only living with these athletes, but chairman of the Consultant's Committee that dealt with both their personal and political problems.

And I want you to know that the whole incident was another "black herring." It wasn't part of any big effort to make the case for black power at the Games. If you'll remember, the whole "black boycott" that Harry Edwards tried to pull off for that Olympiad fell flatter on its face than a one-legged hurdler, as Dave Albritton used to say.

Sure the newspapers in America kept guessing about it beforehand. But those of us who really were in the know didn't. Because we knew the competitors. We knew there were a couple of wild ones but that almost overwhelmingly the American athletes were most interested in doing what was *really* their thing at Mexico. Like Jimmy Hines, the record-breaking sprint man and new "world's fastest human." He wanted to win at Mexico City and break a record to boot, so that he could get himself a good professional football contract. Or Bob Beamon and Ralph Boston, the champion black broad jumpers. They're sympathetic to the Negro cause, as I am and as I hope everyone is, but they wouldn't have dreamed of copying the Smith-Carlos stuff. The same goes for virtually all the rest, Negro and white. The proof is that there weren't any other incidents.

And there weren't any among the athletes of the other thirty-eight nations there. Think of all those seven thousand plus performers from every nook and cranny of the world, then realize that not one went along with Smith and Carlos, and you'll see what a tempest in a teapot—a broken teapot— the whole thing was. The African athletes in particular showed no sympathy for what John and Tommy did. Kenya's Kip Keino, for example, didn't have time for black-power meetings. He already had the power. He proved it by beating our Jim Ryun in the 1,500 meters in less than three minutes and thirty-five seconds, an amazing speed for that staggering Mexico City altitude, which sent behemoths like Australia's record holder Ron Clarke to the hospital.

The same went for Keino's teammate, Nate Temu, who won the 10,000 meters, and for Mamo Wolde, the Ethiopian who was right behind him. No meetings for them. No warm hellos to Smith and Carlos, either. No hellos at all, as far as I could see. The Africans weren't even friendly with our black athletes. They usually stayed with their own countrymen, but when they didn't they were perfectly at ease with the athletes from other countries, eating or sleeping, talking or laughing, black or white.

There were a few British instigators. England didn't do

too well in the Games and wasn't in many of the finals. I
don't like the idea of "team" totals in the Olympics, but it
is interesting to note that England was in thirteenth place
overall beneath countries like Rumania. And of course there
was one American white militant, Hal Connolly. He had lost
out in his own event, and was with Carlos constantly. Hal
believed that there should be a demonstration at the Games
to dramatize what seemed to him the Negro's plight in America. At one meeting, for instance, he brought up the idea of
dipping our flag as a symbol of black protest.

I asked him if he knew about the tradition of never
letting the flag dip.

He looked confused. Sometimes it's easy to forget that
these are nineteen-, twenty-, twenty-five-year-old kids, most
of whom weren't even born until World War II was over.
But Hal is nearly forty.

I told him about the tradition. I didn't like the Vietnam
War, either, I said, but explained that fighting the Nazis and
the Japanese was something else. That flag he was talking
about was planted on Iwo Jima by men like his father. Iwo
Jima represented a principle—the same principle Hal wanted
to uphold by dipping the flag.

They didn't dip the flag.

Carlos and Smith *did* give the black-power salute, of
course. But even their thoughts at the Olympics weren't
consumed by the race situation. First, they had to worry
about winning. If they didn't get up there on the medalists'
pedestal, they weren't going to be giving any salutes at all.
And Tommy Smith's feat in winning the two hundred meters
took monolithic concentration on that event and nothing
else. It was even more amazing because that afternoon he
pulled a muscle in his groin, one of the more painful in-

juries a sprinter can have. In the beginning, it didn't seem
as though he'd be running the finals at all a few hours later.
But a white physician from Oklahoma named Cooper worked
on him, and Tommy ran. And broke not only the Olympic
record but the world mark.

Tommy is a high-class boy, and I think that much of
what he did at the Games was influenced by John Carlos
and by Tommy's wife, who is really extreme on the subject
of black power. And speaking of wives, there wouldn't have
been any demonstration at all if the Consultant's Committee
hadn't found places for the wives to live. Carlos had brought
his wife Kim, and she was living unauthorized in a segment
of the athletes' quarters. The Olympic Committee was about
to remove her, and I think if she had been sent home, her
husband would have gone with her. Without John, I wonder
if Tommy Smith would have given any Nazi salutes. But I
met with them and then with the Olympic Committee, and
the next day Mrs. Carlos had a place of her own to stay in,
with the Committee paying for it.

So Olympic committees picked up tabs and white doctors healed pulled muscles and as a result Tommy Smith
and John Carlos were able to make sick headlines in every
town in America. Actually, they double-crossed some of their
own black teammates who wanted a more organized, meaningful demonstration, by doing what they did. After it
happened, I met with them to try and stop their expulsion
from the Games. I knew what the Olympic Committee was
going to do, and I realized that unless we could come up
with a pretty good argument, Tommy and John would be
sent packing.

I had hopes they'd be reasonable, Tommy in particular.
But they arrived at the meeting with Hal, who was fanning

the fire. Negro militants always become more militant before white audiences. Carlos lost his cool right away. I kept asking him to tell it to me like it really was so that I could make the Olympic Committee understand. "It don't make no difference what I say or do," Carlos would keep repeating. "I'm lower than dirt, man. I'm black." And every time he said something like that, Hal Connolly just about cheered.

Finally, I got fed up. "You know, Carlos," I yelled, "you talk about Whitey this and Whitey that. Everything's 'get Whitey out of my hair!' But when it comes to the most private kind of meeting of all, here you are with good old Whitey! He goes everywhere you go. Man, *I* can get along without him. How come *you* can't?"

The meeting was over. I went to the Olympic Committee and did what I could. It wasn't enough.

But life went on. In the Olympic village, in fact, the Smith-Carlos dismissal caused hardly a brief murmur among the American athletes. And nothing at all among the rest. Most of them probably didn't know about it and couldn't have cared less if they did, just as the rest of the athletes didn't spend time in 1956 worrying about the Red Chinese withdrawal when the Nationalist China banner was raised over their quarters by mistake.

I realize, of course, that right now the 1968 Olympic Games aren't even a dim memory for most. They're past history. But they *are* history, and the record should be set straight. For the Olympic incidents damaged the image of the Negro athlete in America, and sports are important, so important. Because more than anything else to the kid who starts off poor or underfoot, sports represent the American dream. If a boy can't grow up and make it there, he can't make it anywhere.

Well, a Negro kid *can* make it there, *especially* there. It's no accident that there's a higher percentage of colored major league baseball players than in the population at large. Or that almost half the pro basketball players are black. It isn't because that's the only place they'll let us in, either. No one let Einstein into mathematics because he was Jewish. Or white. And it isn't because we've got "rhythm," either.

It's because we're *making it*.

And yet writer after writer has gotten himself a good buck by editorializing on the "poor Negro's" plight in athletics! The height of it was Jack Olsen's *The Black Athlete: A Shameful Story*. His *was* a shameful story. Not that most of Olsen's facts weren't straight. It's that, maybe unknowingly, he stacked the cards by not giving other key facts. He made black athletes seem like Mortimer Snerds for the white Edgar Bergens. He even used me to prove his point, though I never met the man.

If he had interviewed me about the contrast in sports for the Negro between 1930 and 1970, maybe Olsen would have written a different story. It was also strange, too, that he didn't need to talk to people like Clem Haskins of the Chicago Bulls who studied for his master's degree in the off season and who will tell you how fast things are changing for the better. I found it peculiar that Olsen didn't find out about Lou Brock's florist shop in St. Louis or the hundreds of similar businesses run by black athletes. It isn't just their names that are being used, either, like Jesse Owens Cleaners in 1939. Sure, people like Lou Brock aren't making corsages or trimming plants most of the time, but they have to have the sense to hire the right people and the business acumen to make sure those people are doing right by them. Olsen also might have asked Brock about his stocks and bonds. A book—a set of books—could be written about Negro athletes alone who are making it in a variety of ways just as their white teammates are. But hardly an article has been done on them. All you hear is that there are no colored baseball managers or only one black quarterback.

Olsen's articles and so many others like them remind me of a story Negroes who gamble like to tell. It's about the guy who made $10,000 in the numbers. Everyone in Harlem was talking about him, but no one had seen him for weeks. One day he finally showed up, acting funny.

"I hear you made $10,000 in the numbers, Al!" the first fellow who spotted him said, hurrying over.

"Well," Al answered slowly, "that's not too far off. Just a couple little details different than what you heard."

"What?" a bunch of people asked, crowding around him.

"Waaalll," he drawled, "it wasn't ten thousand. It was twenty."

A gasp swept through the crowd.

"It wasn't numbers, either," he went on. "It was horses." Another gasp of admiration.

Al took a deep breath as they all waited for his next words. "And I didn't make it," he said. "I *lost* it."

So much for what has been written about the "poor Negro athlete" in America today.

But read the writing of Rap Brown or listen to the anger of Edwards or be their victim through handed-down and passed-along version after version of black unrest, and you can understand how the myth of blackthink is threatening to take over. Not that Rap isn't telling it like it is—for *him*.

But are the Rap Browns and Harry Edwardses the truth or the exception? Could it be that they write the books they do and make their kind of speeches exactly because they *are* the exceptions?

The answer to that doesn't just lie in some little story Jesse Owens tells about some people he knows that are representative as far as *he's* concerned. Here are the facts: Every responsible individual or organization that has objectively looked into the situation has come to the conclusion that most black nationalists are a horde of "colored con men," as Pulitzer prize-winning writer Harry Ashmore put it in likening blackthinkers to the White Citizens Council. And there were many, many times more people on the White Citizens Councils of the South than there are black extremists.

Do you know how many Black Muslims there are in this country? The estimates range from 8,000 to 80,000 today. Compare that to nonmilitant organizations. Just consider the Negro woman alone—the 40,000 in the Alpha Kappa Alpha sorority dedicated to encouraging higher scholastic standards among Negroes; or the 3,000,000 in the National Council of Negro Women, who work peacefully for economic and social growth; or the 100,000 in the National Association of Colored Women's Clubs working for better education; or the 175,000 daughters of the Elks working with our young people. With these and so many more like them, how can there possibly be more than two or three percent militants?

The Lou Harris study following Martin's murder proved it. *Even then,* at the Negro's moment of greatest disillusion in this century, less than one black in nine favored any kind of separatism. Less than one in twenty opposed desegregation. From scholarly studies such as the analysis by Johns Hopkins University's James Coleman and the Kerner Commis-

sion surveys to what you can see with your own eyes by
looking around you once you turn off the rantings of a few
soapboxing blackthinkers, the facts are plain. Well in excess
of ninety-five percent of all Negroes are no more militant
than I am. In fact, to most of them, the Harry Edwardses
and Jim Formans are like some newspaper caricatures, the
other side of the image that Stepin Fetchit used to play in
films. As one of my sons-in-law said to me not long ago,
"Where has Rap Brown *been,* man?"

Except that it's not funny.

For it has the majority of whites, *and* Negroes, wondering if underneath every brown skin isn't hate and violence
and revolution. Gunnar Myrdal, the Swedish sociologist who
prophesied American's race crisis a generation ago in *An
American Dilemma,* feels a black revolution in this country
is very unlikely because most blacks recognize underneath
it all that "the fundamental thing about Negroes is that they
are Americans." As a matter of fact, Myrdal believes that
"the Negro middle class is more puritan than the white
middle class."

Dr. Raymond Mack of Northwestern University's Center for Urban Affairs carries this a step further. He thinks
that even Negro rioting among the extremists may be going
out of the picture. Why? Because the Negro is so well off
and getting more well off with each new day.

Yes, the Negro has problems—sometimes terrible problems. But they are almost always *human* problems now, and
who in the hell doesn't have those?

5.

Anatomy
of a Militant

"I'm just doing all this to cop out on the homework."
—Student Demonstrator

Negro militancy and revolution, then, are simply the biggest
of black herrings.

But it isn't enough to say that books by the Cleavers
and speeches by the Stokelys are what set off these huge
hoaxes.

Who really creates them? Why? What does it mean to
this country?

The answer lies in the anatomy of a black extremist, at
the very gut of blackthink.

Billy is in a hospital bed as I write this, blind for life.
He was born in 1946 to lower middle-class parents who

believed that love in the home and education outside it were the keys to just about everything. It's pretty hard to argue with that.

Billy's father worked in a bookstore and read three hours a night after coming home from work. His mother was a department-store clerk studying to be a practicing psychologist. It took her until she was forty-five, but she made it.

Billy was an only child, and his mother knew enough psychology not to spoil him. But when it came to education, she and her husband pulled out all the stops. They had gravitated from a small Midwest town to a large eastern city for better jobs and better schooling for their son. There was one school in the area, an expensive and integrated private institution, that was much better than any other.

So they made application for their nine-year-old boy. They anticipated a struggle paying for it, but Bill was given a full scholarship because of the results of his entrance tests. It seemed that all was right with the world for their little family.

Bill got more than good marks at school. He became well liked and in only his sophomore year of high school was elected president of the student council—an unprecedented honor. But one day in ninth grade something had happened that had started Bill thinking along new lines.

He came up against bigotry. Now that in itself was nothing new. Though his family had lived in a nice, integrated neighborhood for as long as he could remember and though he'd gone to one of the best schools in the country since fourth grade, Bill had heard a "nigger" now and then or seen someone who didn't know any better than to stare at him because his skin was a shade of brown rather than white.

But that was the point. Those who did it didn't know any better. These things never bothered Bill, because he'd been taught, and rightly, that only ignorance breeds prejudice. He even came to feel sorry for people who called him names or stared at him. What's more, they really didn't matter anyway. People like that had never been a part of his world. His parents moved in educated circles with friends of all races, and even if they weren't wealthy, Bill had never been slowed down in any important area of his life because he was a Negro.

By the time he was a freshman, the school had held grade parties for a couple of years where a little dancing went on, but mostly the boys stayed apart from the girls. Then things changed. A number of the fellows in the class started dating, and the first dance of the freshman year was coming up, where each boy was free to ask the girl of his choice. There were two Negro girls in the class. One, Belinda, weighed almost two hundred pounds. She looked like the fifty-year-old cleaning woman that came to Bill's house once a week. The other, Marsha, was all right, except for the thick glasses she wore.

But even if Marsha had been a young Diana Ross, it wouldn't have mattered. Bill had always had a crush on Nancy. Tall, as tall as he was almost, with long blonde hair and a lovely figure, she was a bright girl, but with a beautifully innocent smile and outlook to match. Both her parents were professors at a nearby university, and very liberal. When she had invited Bill to her birthday party the year before, they had welcomed it.

The truth was that Nancy secretly returned Bill's feelings and was hoping with all her heart that he would ask her to the dance now that their chance had come. And Bill was going to—until the day he had study period with his best friend, a white youngster named Ron.

Bill and Ron had finished their homework early and asked the librarian if they could talk in her office. She let them, and once there the conversation inevitably drifted to girls. As with boys that age, they laughed about it and began pairing up unlikely couples, their laughter increasing with each match. Suddenly, Ron turned to Bill with a serious expression on his face.

"You know, Billy, you got it rough for this dance. You sure as hell don't want to take four-eyes, and Belinda—aaah!"

Bill felt as though he had been hit in the back with a sledgehammer. He couldn't talk for a few seconds. Finally he forced a smile and whispered, "Yeah, I got it rough."

"You don't have to whisper," Ron said, "the door is thick."

Bill nodded. "Who are you going to take to the dance, Ron?"

"Probably Nancy," Ron replied easily.

From that moment on, Bill did have it a little rough. He didn't go to the dance, and the bitterness inside him grew quietly over his high school years as he watched Ron and Nancy become steadies.

It didn't happen all at once, though. Bill still went on to academic excellence and was twice voted the most popular fellow in his class. He became the man his basketball team looked to in a tight situation, and one year he led them to a league championship. But inside were the seeds of something else, because deep down now he was haunted by the possibility that the friendly white world he had lived in was only an illusion. The riots and rantings going on around him were becoming more than "current affairs." They were close, part of him. And he was going to become a part of them.

Yet Bill was still pulled the other way, too. If he couldn't date Nancy, if he could never again really enjoy being with Ron, if the world was a different place from what he'd thought it was, it was still a place where he was an athletic hero, the president of the student council and a young man with a big career ahead of him, probably in teaching or even in front of a TV camera.

Bill was graduated from high school and entered one of the top eastern colleges. The first semester there he was third in his class. He would have been first if he hadn't had a professor in sociology who never gave above an 88. He was working just as hard the following semester when Martin Luther King was murdered.

We all know that more than a hundred communities violently erupted, taking dozens of lives, after Martin was killed. But what few people know is what quietly happened to thousands and thousands of young men and women who never made the newspapers—young men like Bill. Martin's death was the fuse for all the things they'd felt but hadn't let get the best of them. It changed them. In Bill's case, his grades plummeted. That summer he got a job with a nearby museum. He'd worked every summer since he was thirteen, and each employer had had a good word for him. This time he was fired in a week and a half for insubordination. His parents were disturbed about it, but they finally decided that Bill must have run into a bad apple. He didn't go back to work.

In his sophomore year at college, Bill's marks were barely high enough to allow him to stay in school. The coach was startled when he decided not to go out for the basketball team. But Bill had joined the most radical student political organization and was spending almost all his spare time in the little room on the top floor of the student union building where they met and published a newspaper.

His sophomore summer Bill devoted himself completely to planning a campaign that would change the entire climate of his university. He was going to ask for curriculum and policy changes, and if they weren't granted, he was going to unleash a series of demonstrations the likes of which no one could imagine.

As I said, he's in the hospital as I write this. He'll never see again. He went from demonstrations to sit-ins and finally became involved in a riot where he got hit too hard across the temple. What most worries the doctor and Bill's parents is whether he'll ever leave that hospital at all. For Bill doesn't seem to want to get well.

Bill is the son of one of my good friends. His mother pleads, "Where did we go wrong?" His father tells me, "I just don't understand how this happened." But I think I understand. And I wonder if Bill did go wrong.

For I'm not condemning every extremist. I can't agree with every single thing that Billy did, yet I feel there's got to be a place for the strongest kind of dissent in our society. More important, there's got to be a place—an important place—for dissenters like the Bills in particular. So I'd be the very last to tell you about him to make the low point that every militant comes to a tragic end. There's no heavy-handed moral here. What happened to Bill is horrible. What he did, to the largest extent at least, was healthy and necessary. Bill was brought up to feel that the world was his apple. When he suddenly felt the personal meaning of the statistics he'd memorized in school—twice as many Negroes as whites unemployed, mixed marriages and mixed friendships hardly ever working, the children of blacks dying in infancy many times as often as whites—there would have been something very wrong with him if he hadn't reacted.

I know what you're thinking. I can't help being tempted by it, too. Maybe Bill could have risen above it all and asked Nancy to the dance? Maybe she and her parents would really have accepted him and they'd have gone on to a fine marriage and Bill to a professorship in some university? Maybe he would have sidestepped all the bitterness and tragedy that was to be his?

Maybe.

But *maybe* is shaky stuff where a thirteen-year-old boy is concerned. If it weren't for the grace of a couple of people, it would have been much too shaky for me, too.

I know exactly what Bill felt because I felt it—the entire year before I entered college. It was one thing to know the terror of Oakville, but you could leave Oakville behind. Yet the thing that really made Oakville what it was for all of us, the power of a white man over my father—the economic power, the authority to make our supper table empty and the threat to throw us out on the street to die—was part of Cleveland too.

My father simply couldn't get steady work. He tried hard, but he didn't have a skill to his name except for planting cotton. No, we didn't starve, though hunger was something you lived with like you lived with the color of your skin. We didn't starve or get thrown out of our house, because my mother hired out while my sister took care of the baby, because Prentis and Quincy and Sylvester always worked, because even I held three jobs, though sometimes for pennies.

We didn't starve, but we sure didn't prosper. And the constant fear that we lived with down South was still with us, in the back of our minds most of the time now instead of the front, but there, big as night. The white man still controlled my father, only this time it was many white men— the people who didn't have a job for him.

While in East Technical High School, I broke the record in the hundred-yard dash, running it in 9.4 seconds. I'd been coming close, but until I actually did it no one noticed me much. Once it happened, though, the whole world seemed to be at my door. Reporters wanted interviews, and even long-distance calls came to the school for me.

But then the real stuff began to happen. Colleges started sending letters. Some of them even sent people. Everyone wanted me to go to his university. At *his* cost. Many of them were willing to have me live in high style, in fact. One school offered me not only my own six-room apartment off the campus and a new car but "use" of two beautiful women whenever I wanted.

Colored, of course.

But that wasn't the real rub. I was already married (though hardly anyone knew it) and not looking for the use of any beautiful women. I was looking to make sense of a scene that was tearing me apart. I would be invited to eat lobster in the hotel rooms of the men who came to town from the different universities when I didn't even know how to get it out of the shell. Then I'd come home to see my family at a dinner table that didn't look as good as a white man's garbage can.

The gap was too great. I wanted to break out—I wanted to break out and run so fast from the poverty and the ignorance that I'd never have to look back at it again. But not if I had to walk over my sisters and brothers and mother and father to do it. How could school after school dare to offer me what could cost thousands of dollars a year for four entire years while my father had just been laid off a job loading hundred-pound crates that paid him $12 for a sixty-hour week?

But it wasn't just out of loyalty that I turned them all down. It was out of fear. I was scared shitless of moving into a world where I would live like a millionaire while my father nearly starved. In that kind of world, I could be starving tomorrow, too.

At the same time I hated to say no to those offers. Damn, how I hated it. I wanted to believe in the American dream. Part of me had always believed in it. So I began to go to pieces inside, one piece at a time, as the months passed and the records I broke and kept on breaking only kept underlining the hurt of it all. In its own way it was a worse letdown than what I'd experience after the 1936 Olympics. Because here it was as though my success was responsible somehow for my father's failure. It seemed to me almost that I was going to be held accountable for what happened to every poor Negro.

The pressure gathered inside me like an Alabama tornado. Of course, there was no university president's office to sit in then, no marches to join. If there had been, there were days when I would have been leading them.

What I did do was to protest in the only way I knew how. I quit the track team.

Everyone who knew me and those who only knew about

me were shocked. Jesse Owens giving up track! Without it
I was like every other Negro—less than nothing.

But with it, I was a white man's Negro, climbing on
my own father's back to go to a white man's college while
he and my family were starved by other white men.

So I went to coach Charles Riley one morning, chok-
ingly thanked him for everything he had done—and he had
done just about everything at times—and told him I wouldn't
be back.

I was miserable after that. Going along was tempting.
Only *I* knew how tempting. I'd begun to hate my family and
every black man on earth for what I felt I had to do for them.
For the first time in my life I'd openly disobeyed my mother
and swore at my father, storming out of the house after a
visit and not seeing them for ten days. Ruth and I hadn't
spoken a word to each other in three days.

But I quit. The system wasn't going to make a novocain
nigger out of me.

The offers kept coming in. I tore them up in a temper.
When representatives arrived at our two-room apartment,
Ruth told them I wasn't there. If she couldn't convince them,
I came to the door myself and slammed it in their faces.
Gradually, the offers began to trickle away. And my future
with them.

One day at school Charles Riley took me aside. "Jesse,
you know I respect you for what you're doing," he said. "But
if I could get your father a job, a permanent job, would you
go to college—on *your* terms, I mean?"

"There are no permanent jobs for *Negroes*, Mr. Riley," I
answered.

"But if there were?" he said.

"Sure."

"Will you keep up your studies in the meantime? And work out? Not run in competition—just stay in shape?"

I nodded slowly.

"I'll see you around, buddy," he said. *Buddy* was what I always called people to show affection.

Charles Riley motored to Ohio State University that weekend. He met with the best college track coach in the country, Larry Snyder. He told Snyder that he wanted me to go to Ohio State, first because it was really where I belonged and second because he respected Larry's coaching ability.

"But we can't compete with all the other colleges Owens has been getting offers from," Snyder said. "We don't even give athletic scholarships here."

"He doesn't want a scholarship," Riley answered. "He'll work while he goes to school. All he wants is for his father to have a job. For good."

Snyder nodded and a grin began to widen his mouth. "I see," he answered. "Let me talk to some alumni I know. Can you wait a couple of hours?"

"I can wait a couple of days," Riley told him.

Sunday night Charles Riley knocked on the door of our apartment. In his hand was a letter from the dean's office at Columbus. They wanted me to attend college there. They also offered me three jobs. If I waited tables, worked in the library and ran an elevator seven days a week, I could pay off my tuition and board and modestly support my family.

Riley also had another letter. It said that my father was offered a permanent job with the state of Ohio. I was five inches taller than he was, but I threw my arms around Charles Riley and kissed him.

Riley, a shy, bespectacled little fellow who looked kind of like the late Barry Fitzgerald, was a rare man, as much a father to me as Henry Owens was. It was he who saw my potential when I was hardly healthy enough to run to the corner for a newspaper. And that was just the beginning. He saved me from the sickness of blackthink, 1930 style. He was the first white man I really knew and, without ever trying, he proved to me beyond all proof that a white man can understand—and love—a Negro. I don't have to say how much I loved him.

Charles Riley was rare, but there are others like him. And there's a bit of him in so many men. Yet the black-thinkers of today reject this. They even damn the Rileys for trying to help. I'm not talking about the professional liberals who get rid of their guilts or swell their faltering egos by supporting the cause. I'm talking about the *real* liberals, like Charles Riley.

And the militants I'm referring to are very different from Billy, too. Their views may sometimes be the same as his, they may even belong to the same organizations. But their style is a far cry from that of the honest extremists, because their motivation is so different. Except for the ones like Billy, black power is plaything, profit-thing or ego-thing to those who, faced with the job of building their own characters, cop out and "build a new world" instead.

To Ted, a twenty-year-old Negro sophomore at a California University, it's plaything. Ted is the younger brother of one of my son-in-law's acquaintances. He goes to college, he says, to learn how to carry on a dialogue someday in the right way. But instead of learning, he simply has "dialogues" all the time right now—the wrong way. Rather than going to classes, he goes to meetings. What classes he does attend he disrupts by spouting the "history and philosophy of the future" instead of learning real history and philosophy so that he can put his own ideas in perspective.

But the truth is that there's no new philosophy in Ted's future. When he leaves college (and he may do that prematurely, because his marks are bad), his demonstrating days will be a thing of the past. He might go on to an even more undisciplined way of life as some kind of half-hippie, but chances are he'll just get a little-less-than-ordinary job and dissolve into society. He'll never be really satisfied with his life, and once in awhile may become involved in some cause for a few weeks—like whether his neighborhood should be rezoned or should America have a new antimissile system. But only for a few weeks. He'll probably talk about his college days every chance he gets, as though they were some kind of golden period where the youth of this country was "making over this stinking world."

Ted doesn't actually have any philosophy, new or old. He changes his views on issues as fast as a different extremist leader can lay a hand on his shoulder and blow in his ear. He's in the majority as far as today's militants are concerned but, majority or not, he's still a hanger-on. And the reason he's going along for the ride is that it's the *easy* way. One vacation he said it to his brother in a rare moment of honesty. "Chuck," he confided, "I'm just doing all this to cop out on the homework. And sometimes I hate myself for it."

Yet when Ted goes back to school, his self-hate will turn itself outward, against teachers who've spent a lifetime in intellectual pursuits, against fellow students who only want an education, against a society that is pretty rotten in places but for which he really has nothing better to substitute.

His mother is very disturbed about him. She has to work

so that, with Ted's father's job, they can have the money to send him away to school and still take care of the rest of the family. More than once she's urged her husband to pull him out of college. "We can't do that," he tells her. "He's getting something from it. It's not Ted, it's the whole generation. Inside, I think he knows he's drifting. He'll come out of it."

If I were Ted's dad, I'd have him out of school in five minutes. Not because of the demonstrations, but because of his marks. Yet I have to agree with his father that Ted's behavior is only part of a larger youth rebellion that happens every so often. That doesn't mean I'm writing off what's happening now simply as inevitable adolescent behavior. The teen and college rebellion of today is very important and different than it ever has been before. One reason it's so important is that it points up to me and my generation just how badly we've "succeeded." One reason it's different is that this country has never before had a certain kind of militant who would lead and goad and push the Bills and Teds over the brink.

Militants like B.

Not long ago I was speaking at a big college in the New York area. Afterward, I walked across the campus to where a fairly well-known black militant was also giving a speech. He was ranting and raving and had the audience on their feet ranting and raving much of the time. For a minute, I was actually afraid they were going to march out of that hall and tear down the school.

But the speaker knew just how to quiet them whenever things got to the pressure point. His words would go soft and honey-dipped, he'd stop still and a few seconds later the audience would be like a group of statues. I could only take it for about fifteen minutes, then went outside for a breath of air. Just as soon as I loosened my tie, a young Negro came through the doors and walked over to me.

"You're Jesse Owens, aren't you?"

I nodded.

"Slumming?"

"I like to hear all sides," I said.

I think he could see I meant it, and he softened. We stood there talking for almost half an hour. I'm not going to say I made a convert. Because there was no converting to do. He was right-hand man for B, and he no more thought that "black power" could solve America's problems than I believed the right detergent could wash out prejudice.

"It's a living," he said to me. "A damned good living. And it's not a bad cause. Though sometimes I think he and the rest go too far." He told me the take for their last six appearances, all made within two weeks' time. The admissions never ran below two dollars a head, and they hadn't drawn fewer than two hundred people wherever they went. Their expenses for these one-night stands were next to nothing. Dozens of students were just itching to have B. at their homes or pay his way at one of the better hotels around.

"And you should see the contributions that come in," he grinned. "I get three hundred a week and you meet a lot of sweet chicks traveling around the country like this. But I'd rather be in for just a straight ten percent."

"What does B. do with the bucks?" I asked.

"Are you kidding?" came the answer. "He's got bank accounts in seven states. If he doesn't retire before he hits forty, I'm Bill Buckley."

None of this was news to me. Not one white man in a hundred thousand can retire at forty. But a number of

Negroes today are finding a way through blackthink. Some of them will even make it by thirty, in fact. Some of them *have* made it.

This doesn't mean that just any sepia-skinned golden voice with a couple of years of college can turn the trick. The wealthy militants are almost always highly educated, and sometimes very original thinkers. I admire their minds if not their characters. Right or wrong, Eldridge Cleaver has something to say. And few people understand how very much Malcolm X had to say at the end, when he turned away from blackthink.

I also don't mean that every militant of this type is interested only in the money. Many may have believed what they had been saying for some time and simply found a way to make it profitable. But it does beat full-time teaching or sit-ins or any other "ings" or "ins." People cheering you wherever you go. Seeing your name in the newspapers. Speaking maybe twice a week for five hundred dollars an appearance and relaxing or reading or balling the rest of the time.

Still, even if an important group of the militant leaders are opportunists or idealists who sold out, I'm not trying to make devils out of them. I don't see any real difference in selling ideas you don't believe or in selling refrigerators or deodorants you don't dig. I guess racing against scared horses isn't much different, either. It's something most of us do. It's also something we should grow out of.

But you might be thinking: how many leaders can there be? There can't be more than a small number of blacks who command five hundred dollars an appearance or demand fifty thousand dollars for making a book out of their speeches.

And there *is* only a small number. Yet just as important is the blackthink that has become a profit-thing to many, many more people than those few who expect to be millionaires—from the printers who publish the pamphlets to the politicians who use blackthink to get votes.

To the looters.

Do you really think that the rioters who grab the television sets and the vacuum cleaners from shattered store windows during riots are black revolutionaries? The revolutionaries are almost always cool calculators who plan the thing, set it off and know every expert technique to keep it going. But the rioters themselves? They want the television sets and vacuum cleaners. Militancy is the excuse that lets them take these things. Some of them would've broken in anyway and stolen those goods, the others would've looked longingly at them day after day and only wanted to do it.

Of course, a riot serves a psychological purpose for these people too. It lets them blow the hostility that has gathered in them, not against whites, but against a world that asked them to get up at seven in the morning and put in eight good hours in order to have the things they want.

So from the lowest looter to the highest sounding race profiteer, blackthink for money isn't pretty. To its dollar-hungry pitchmen, it's like a kid's chemistry set in which someone has mistakenly supplied the chemicals in full potency. Yet even the blackthinking profit-prophets don't chill my bones like another kind of militant, the one who *has* to do what he's doing, not because he believes in it and is honestly turned on like the Billys or even because he doesn't believe in anything and is drifting aimlessly like the Teds.

But because he's sick.

Lonnie was born in the forties in a poor section of Chicago. I guess you'd have to call it a ghetto. He never knew his father, who was only a one-night affair for his mother. He had one younger brother and an older sister, the three of them from three different men.

Lonnie's mother hated her children because they reminded her of her unhappy episodes with the male sex and because the youngsters were a burden to her. She didn't do much to assume that burden, though. Most of the time she was at one of the bars down the street getting drunk and trying to pick herself up a date. The older girl became responsible for the boys from the beginning. When Sissy wasn't able to handle it, her mother would beat the three of them when she came home.

One night Sissy couldn't handle the responsibility at all. Her mother had left a cigarette burning beside the bed. It fell onto the floor where there were some newspapers, spread to the other room and trapped the children. A fire engine was finally called by one of the neighbors, but by that time Sissy and little Jim were burned to death. Lonnie survived, with horrible scars he'd always have to live with.

His mother was jailed then, and Lonnie was put in an orphan home. Now he lived in a world where no one cared at all, where there wasn't even a Sissy. He ran away from that world about once a month from the very beginning, but he'd be found, brought back, whipped and thrown into a form of solitary confinement.

When Lonnie was thirteen he ran away, hitched a ride on a freight car and was never brought back. He'd planned it carefully, and two hours later was in another state. From there he begged what food he could and kept catching freight cars until he was in a place, California, where he could just about live outside (or in underground garages) twelve months a year. For the first year he was there, he had to do just that.

Then he met an older man who introduced him to homosexuality. By doing what the man wanted he could stop living in underground parking lots. But the man gave him more than room and board. Even though it was in a perverted fashion, this was the first person to care about Lonnie since his older sister. So the boy came to depend on it. By the time he was fifteen, Lonnie was a full-fledged homosexual.

The older man was educated and had a circular room lined with books. Lonnie learned to read them, and once he had started, never stopped. He lived there almost two years, reading and submitting to every perversion that has probably ever been in any book. Then one day the man was jailed for another offense and Lonnie was left homeless again.

But he was old enough to make it on his own now. It took him seven years from the time he was eighteen, but Lonnie finally entered and graduated from college. During those years he also found a cause, a cause in which he could have the love of a lot of people at once and in which he could lead them by expelling the hate that had gathered inside him for twenty-four years.

As I write this, Lonnie has been a leader in one facet of the black-power movement for quite a while. When he speaks, he's articulate and scholarly. Over the past decade he's read thousands of books and countless articles. When he spews hate, virtually no one realizes it's only because of what happened to him personally. Lonnie talks about building a better world, but that's only a thin platitude to disguise what he really wants to do: *destroy this world, which destroyed part of him.* He ends a lot of speeches with, "Make love, not war," and then sneaks off to seduce some eighteen-year-old black boy who idolizes him.

Lonnie is extremely ill and is an extreme example of one influential segment of today's militants, a segment that includes dope addicts, criminals, and deviates. Lonnie is all these: he is on speed, he once stole as a way of life, and he is a confirmed homosexual.

But one thing he isn't. He is not motivated by what Negro psychologist Kenneth B. Clark calls "a genuine Negro fear of moving outside the 'pathetically protective' walls of segregation."

Because Lonnie isn't Negro.

He is white. His parents were white. There isn't any more Negro blood in his body than there is in George Wallace's.

Still, he attracts Negroes—both to his cause and to his bed. Because he knows what the most downtrodden Negro feels and has felt. If any black-power advocate ever tells you that a white man can't understand what it's like to experience what some Negroes have in America, don't believe him.

Lonnie knows.

The stories of Billy, Ted, B. and Lonnie can only be sketches at best. Even then, to generalize from the most representative of sketches is risky. People are complex and are individuals. That's one of the things this book is all about.

But something is true of every one of us, even a pathetic, driven, broken person like Lonnie.

We have a choice.

No, not the choice of becoming a Martin Luther King. Our past experiences and our capacities take that option away almost from the start. But there's a more important choice that nothing or no one but you can ultimately take away from yourself.

Whether to *really* battle the prison you find yourself in, or give in.

Violence, hate and self-pity are easy.

Self-control, true assertiveness and long-range planning are the challenges of a different color.

Think for a minute about Ted and Lonnie and B.

Escaping from cracking the books so as to crack heads.

Making a point only to make a buck.

Changing the world so you don't have to change yourself.

Put them together. Now you see it like it truly is. Now you know who's copping out where really fighting whitethink is concerned.

The militants are the *real* Uncle Toms.

6.

Blackthink
Won't Win

> . . . I was full of hate, just full, and not only for
> the white man, but for every living thing. No one
> can go on like that."
> —Roderick Thorp in *Dionysus*

"The great demonstration strengthens the individual . . .
the man who is exposed to serious oppression needs that
strengthening . . . justification of using the most brutal
weapons always depends on the presence of a fanatical
belief in the necessity of the victor, of a revolutionary new
order. . . . The most striking success will always be won
whenever the new view is taught to all people, and if necessary, is forced upon them. . . ."

The credo of a leading black revolutionary? Bits of
speeches by black militants?

There are two answers to those questions. The first is

yes, in a sense. For, give or take an adjective or a comma, almost all of the black extremists of today have made statements nearly identical to the one you have just read. But the second answer is *no,* the quotation did not come from any American militant. It was written by Adolf Hitler in *Mein Kampf.*

As I said, I'm no scholar in history, but I don't think you have to be a Ph.D. to see the striking, disgusting similarity between all forms of tyranny. Suppressing the personal identity of the individual into some group, the end justifying the means, force instead of freedom. These are what makes every despot and potential despot tick, whether it be a Hitler, a George Lincoln Rockwell, a KKK'er or a black militant. Long before they invade any place on a map, something has invaded them, something deadly. I've seen black extremism eat up men, devouring their minds and actions one chunk at a time in much the same way they want to do it to society. I've seen the despotism of the spirit drive out almost everything else good in a man, day after day, sometimes hour by hour, until he's a fanatic wooden stereotype.

Oh, he begins by hating the white man. But hate is a tricky thing. It's malignant. The black militants I've known all ended up hating much more than the white man—their own women, families, closest friends. For, deep down, they *must* hate everyone.

You can't go on like that. No way. Except the "way" that really isn't a way at all: to keep refueling the cancer, giving it more and more to feed on. Now it's spread through your own body, so give it other bodies. Riot. Loot. Hurt. Kill. Drown out those dim noises inside you with shouts and the crackling of flames and guns.

So the first "fruit" of blackthink is what it does to those who give in to it. But spiritual self-destruction is *only* the beginning. Blackthink has even destroyed a part of millions of Negroes who are a hundred percent against it by leading them to believe that their brothers secretly feel hate for the white.

Whatever *you've* been led to believe, Negroes are not a monolithic group. Brown skin doesn't signify something mystical where we all know what our next-door neighbor is thinking, let alone thinking the same thing as he is. It pains me to give the blackthinkers the satisfaction of saying it, but, though they've failed miserably at converting the Negro people to their extremism, they've been all too effective in convincing blacks that somewhere, somehow, a lot of other blacks are silent sympathizers.

One thing I want to accomplish in this book is to still the fear, of both whites and Negroes, that if and when the extremists try anything really wild, there'll be millions upon millions of black bronze faces streaming out of the woodwork of our cities to join in. For blackthink has destroyed the confidence of the white and Negro in each other, and next to this, the destruction of property is almost unimportant.

Blackthink gives the obvious white bigot a platform he never had before. The quiet white racist is supplied with an unspoken "proof" of his own prejudices. The average white, who really isn't too involved in race except where it touches him, becomes irritated with it all. But most important, the essentially unprejudiced white, the genuine liberal who has spent part of his life battling for the Negro in one way or another, is crushed. After all these years, he's suddenly "Whitey"; he's on the outside looking in. And if he looks in too long, he might wind up in the hospital.

The most diseased example of this is the wave of anti-Semitism among militant blacks today. To me, it's just a final demonstration of the sickness of blackthink—one more parallel between blackthink and Nazism. I mean, why the Jews? They're a minority just like us, and a minority who went through hell even longer.

And *that's* why the militants hate them. Because the Jews did go through it all, and survived. Blackthinkers don't hate the Jews because they own some slum buildings (a lot of Protestants do, too, and many more Negroes—as I'll go into later), or because a lot of Jews have colored maids, or because the Jews have been the leaders in the "tokenism" civil rights movement of the fifties and sixties.

The blackthinkers are anti-Semitic because so many Jews did what the militants don't want to do. They've overcome. That doesn't sit well when you've copped out yourself.

It wouldn't hurt the black militants to remember that Hitler felt the same about Negroes as he did about Jews. Before our Olympic track team entered Berlin in 1936, the German papers ran stories about how we were subhuman and wouldn't be any competition for Hitler's master race. After our Negro athletes took seven out of eleven track and field events, the Nazi papers sour-graped how "black auxiliary tribes" had unfairly participated. For myself, before or after wasn't as frustrating as the competition itself. Hitler treated me as if I were some kind of animal.

And the bitterest irony of all is the way that black-think would chain the Negro while touting freedom to him. "They're coming over to our way of thinking," Black Muslim

Cassius Clay said of the non-Muslim Negro extremists a couple of years ago. And they are. Militants are asking not for a better education, for example, but for a black education, with black teachers and black dormitories. Jim Crow schools, in other words. From "Black Easter" to the "New Republic of Black Africa," it's the same principle. Segregation. Sure, the window dressing is nicer now, but it's still going back to where we were.

Yet the mental self-destruction, the anti-Semitism, even the Jim Crowism and the actual damage to life and property, none of it scares me as much as one thing that blackthink is doing to this country. *It is conditioning us to use violence to solve our problems.*

Let me say straight out that I don't believe in non-violence. More than once Martin Luther King, Jr. and I disagreed on this. I say if a man hits you, you sometimes must hit back. If a sadist comes to your home and threatens your family, you may have to kill him.

Each man has a right, a responsibility, to defend his own life. Freedom is unfortunately sometimes the freedom to use violence—only after you've first been attacked in some way. But prejudice isn't violence. I'm not saying bigotry isn't rotten. But the line between the man who pulls a gun on me and the bigot who pulls a prejudice against me is a thick line. And if we handle them both the same way, we're trading liberty for the jungle. The fellow who thinks Negroes are inferior and won't have anything to do with them is stupid, maybe sick. But in the United States he has a right to be those things as long as he doesn't back up his ideas as the KKK or the blackthinkers have—with fists and fires and ropes. I think that's what this country is all about. Oh, you can make people sell their houses to buyers they don't want and seat in their restaurants customers they'd ordinarily keep out, but you can't pass a law against prejudice.

What's more, you *shouldn't*. What in the hell is liberty if you make everyone else think the way you do? The blackthinkers, sometimes unconsciously, sometimes deliberately, are trying to take away that liberty. They don't educate, they don't persuade. Their "dialogues" are usually a hoax. They believe in violence to solve problems. They've used it before, they're threatening it continually, they're planning it for tomorrow.

Sometimes they'll talk with you. But in the background is the gun and the knife, the riot and the revolution. It's no *discussion* when one debater holds a pistol in his hand and says, "If we don't do it this way, we'll do it *this* way."

I have confidence that we're going to lick this thing, that the overwhelming majority in America and the new generations coming up will whip both white bigots and blackthinkers alike. But if I have one fear for my country, it's that we're becoming more and more used to seeing violence "solve" problems and are getting closer and closer to thinking that some kind of a revolution is inevitable.

Blackthink isn't one hundred percent bad. It was born partly out of Negro pride, and one of its effects has been a white awakening. But even if the militants were right about every single thing they advocate, the means they're using and threatening to use to win their ends would make it all worthless. Lerone Bennett, Jr., told how one peace-loving Harlem woman reacted to the riots: ". . . hearing the guns I felt like something was crawling in me, like the whole damn world was no good. . . . And I took this pop bottle and it was empty and I threw it down on the cops, and I was crying and laughing."

Fifty-seven years on this earth have shown me that men aren't basically evil. But they aren't basically good, either. The possibilities for both are always in us, and just because we did the right thing on Tuesday and Wednesday doesn't mean we're sure to do it on Friday and Saturday. You can't rest on your laurels where character is concerned, just as you can't stop breathing and expect to live simply because you've drawn fifty million breaths before that. Humanity isn't something you're given. It isn't a natural state of being. You earn it. You've got to work to be human.

The woman who threw the pop bottle at the policeman is a lot of women. But for every one of her, there are dozens who don't throw anything. They're the ones I care about, and worry about, the ones who hold themselves in and fight the battle where it's really at. Inside themselves. Because with each passing hour, many of them are coming close to feeling that they're fighting for very little, that it's a violent world where only violence will work. And it's this feeling that creates a seething Satan inside them. There's no devil there to begin with. Doubt and disillusion putrifying from ignorance—that's what produces the animal in us.

I came close to violence a number of times, both as man and boy. There was that time with that Indiana restaurant owner who would've starved us if he'd had his way. And the days after Martin was shot. But there have been other times. The one I remember most was in 1940, when Joe Louis and I were in a bar together in Chicago.

Joe and I had been lucky to come along at a time when the imagination of the American public at large was ready to be captured by Negro athletes. Because of this, we had unique roles to play in our culture, and it welded us together as friends. Our lives crossed only several times a year, but we understood each other from the beginning.

One night after a banquet, a bunch of guys asked us to a nearby lounge for some further celebration. Neither Joe nor I were drinkers, but we sat around and jawed with reporters and friends. The bar was crowded, and mixed.

As soon as we sat down, we were recognized. With me, people usually just said hello and asked for an autograph. But with Joe it was different, because he was heavyweight boxing champion. Everyone wanted to throw a punch at him. It was like a ritual. They'd throw it, not hard enough to hurt but fast enough to make contact. Then they'd be able to say that they had "hit Joe Louis." But they never got to say it. Like lightning Joe would block the blow just before it reached him. Then they'd nod their heads in admiration, shake his big bear hand and walk away satisfied that Joe was indeed the best in the world.

Only this night it wasn't like that. From across the room came a white man almost Joe's size and thicker across the chest. He walked slowly until he caught our eye, then posed in a boxing stance to let Joe know he wanted to go through the same ritual countless men had before. Only this guy didn't have a smile on his face. When he got up to our table, he said, "You're Joe Louis, aren't you?"

Joe nodded shyly. He never did get used to being famous.

"Mind if I throw one at you?" the guy asked.

Joe stood up. "Go ahead, pal."

The man tossed his left toward Joe's gut, and Joe's right arm shot out to block the punch. Joe thought it was all over when his forearm made contact with the fellow's fist, and he began to turn to sit down.

But the left had only been a feint. The instant Joe was

off guard, the big fellow's right came up and smashed into his chin and neck. Joe went reeling against a wall and almost instinctively came out fighting a couple of seconds later.

I grabbed his hands. He knew they were deadly weapons in the eyes of the law, but I still reminded him.

I kept myself between Joe and the guy. A crowd had gathered around us. "What'd you do that for, mister?" I yelled.

I can't remember all that he said. He began with having his "nigger for the week" and went on from there to just about every obscenity I'd ever heard. He was obviously sick, for some reason full of hate against the Negro, a hate he no doubt had to let out now and then or else.

He hated Joe Louis in particular. Through some mental process that only a psychiatrist could explain, Joe had upset this white man's notion of the way things should be.

It was a bad scene. The other whites had gathered behind their champion, and all the Negroes were standing behind me and Joe. As each cuss word spewed out of the man's twisted face, I felt the crushing injustice of what was being done to the Negro in America. I felt what every black man felt who ever walked into a bar or a diner and saw only one empty seat, between two white men—the shame of automatically wondering, "Am I imposing? Will it be all right?" Because, let's face it, it's the *white man's* bar. And then there's the self-hate, and the bitterness against all whites you feel because you *do* have a right to sit there, too. I felt what every Negro feels when he walks into a store in a white neighborhood and the counter girls and customers all secretly ask themselves whether he's there to rob or to buy something. I felt the monstrous insecurity and then the almost hysterical resentment. And I hated this sonofabitching white man for all of it. No, I didn't expect a world without psychos in it. But why did so many of the psychos have to be hung up on Negroes?

Even then, I'd gone through the same kind of scene before, and it hadn't made me knock out anybody's teeth. What I hadn't seen was that kind of sickness directed against Joe Louis, one of the two or three men I'd known with a completely pure soul. Nature had made Joe big and strong and extraordinarily well-coordinated. But he was also the complete good guy, a man who'd spent all his life letting people walk over him and only hoping they didn't trip as they did it. He's still doing the same today. Like me, Joe didn't have Martin's brain, yet that made his goodness stand out even more. No one in this world but a maniac crammed with hate could have wanted to hurt Joe Louis.

I didn't want to hurt that white man. I wanted to kill him.

I honestly wasn't aware that I'd grabbed a beer mug and smashed it jagged against the table top. I only knew that suddenly I was standing inches from the bastard with a lethal weapon raised above his face.

He cowered backward a little and then went still as a statue. Someone started to rush in to stop me, but I shouted him back with a savage threat. Everyone stayed where they were. Voices were saying things to me, but they were like the shouts you hear when you're in the middle of a race. You only hear the noises, not what they're saying. I was listening to what was inside me, and I didn't have to listen long. I knew what was there—the same thing that's inside all blackthinkers.

Revenge. Revenge for everything that ever went wrong in their lives, revenge against someone who's had it better.

My life had been better than most Negroes'. But my father's hadn't, nor my brothers' and sisters', nor the brother's and sister's who never lived because there were no doctors for sharecroppers' babies.

I wanted revenge for their sake and, to be brutally honest, for never having been able to enjoy my good fortune completely because of them. I can't tell you how much I wanted to kill that white man. More than I had wanted to win at Berlin.

I didn't touch him. Not because I'm any saint. Far from it. Simply because there was something in me weighing even heavier than the revenge.

But for some Negroes today, particularly the younger ones, there sometimes isn't anything heavier inside. You can analyze the militant from now till the twenty-first century, break him down into ego-thinker, profit-thinker, play-thinker or anything else, but what's beneath *that?* Why the race issue for fun or profit or false pride?

Revenge, that's why.

Maybe a story that went around a few years ago tells it best. You might have heard it, yet I doubt whether you gave it much thought, really understood it, felt its meaning in your bones. It's about the black man and white man, both members of a chain gang in the South. Every day for eight years they've been working together, breaking the rocks, fixing the roads, hating their boss. Through it all, the two have become closer than a white and a black have ever become, closer than brothers. So they plan an escape together.

The day comes. Everything is to go off like clockwork, for they've been in this one area for months. At exactly noon a train always goes by a half-mile from where they are, on its way nonstop through the state and to freedom. They figure it'll take them three minutes to run that half-mile through the field and barely make the train. So at exactly ten minutes before noon, they'll knock out the boss with a pipe they've hidden, break their chains and race toward the railroad track.

Everything goes perfectly. At exactly ten to twelve they lay the boss low, and several minutes later their chains are broken and they're on their way. But the sheriff is passing by at that moment, sees what has happened and takes off with his gun in hand after the two.

They seem to have the lead they need, though. They race across fields and through streams, the Negro slightly ahead, until they're only a hundred yards from the track. But the train is almost there, speeding along at seventy miles an hour, twirling around the bend, now flashing in front of their eyes in the noon sun, threatening to pass. The two men race for it, the voice of the sheriff yelling, "Stop or I'll shoot!" in back of them while the wheels of the train whirl in front of them. With their final bursts of breath, they lunge for the very last car as it rockets out of reach. They strain, and strain again with everything in them.

And the colored man grabs on!

The white man keeps running, reaching out for the now outstretched arm of the Negro, but the train is moving away from him by inches, then by feet and finally for good. And as it pulls away with the Negro safely on it and the white man now under the sheriff's gun, the black feels an overpowering desire to say something to his friend, to this

man who has been like a brother to him for eight years
and has seemed to have grown closer to him than he ever
thought a white man could.

He knows exactly what he wants to say, too. A big
smile forms on his face, he sets his teeth together and
he yells, "See yooooooooooo, Whitey!"

Some of the greatest truths about the race problem *are*
spoken in jest. And this is the truth of blackthink. The
militants who flaunt guns and foment revolution aren't
motivated by high-sounding ideals like justice or brother-
hood, they aren't even looking to help the blacks, but only
to hurt the whites. What's more, they aren't against bigotry.
They are the bigots. What sociologist Calvin Hernton said
of the works of Negro playwright LeRoi Jones makes too
much sense: "There is all the hatred, venom, brutality,
profanity and downright insanity that whites have tradi-
tionally heaped upon the Negro."

A short time ago I was watching one of the many
discussions by Negroes about Negroes on TV. The subject
was the black ghetto. I wouldn't say the panel was well-
balanced. All were militants, and it really seemed that the
only question was who could outdo who in heaping blame
and bitterness on whites. Finally they came to vice and
prostitution. One rash statement followed another. Eventually, a student leader said, "You see, it isn't enough for
the white man to emasculate our males. He has to make
whores out of our women!"

I know one of those whores. Her name is Barbara.
I've known her since she was a child. Her father is an
acquaintance of mine, working in the city of Chicago, coming home to his wife and family each night as he has been
for the twenty-nine years of his marriage. When he walks

in the door now, though, there is a deep sadness in the house, for both he and her mother know what Barbara is.

They didn't make her that way. Her brothers and sisters, all of whom are now happily married, didn't make her that way. The "ghetto" they lived in didn't make her that way. Above all, the white man didn't make her that way.

Barbara was always a beautiful girl, but in her teens she was presented with the same set of choices other girls are. She made the wrong ones. First she was simply "fast" with the boys her own age. Then the boys her own age weren't fast enough. She began dating older men, and soon dating only the men who had the means to give her expensive gifts. Gradually, the gifts became necessities. Gradually, Barbara became a high class call girl.

Today she's not a high class anything. The last I heard of her was four months ago on Sixty-third Street. Her pimp didn't recognize me, and tried to solicit business for Barbara. The last time I saw her was two years ago at a demonstration outside a south side factory. Her beauty was almost gone, and the sleeves of her dress couldn't completely cover the needle marks on her arm. At twenty-four, she looked closer to forty. She didn't notice me. She was too busy screaming curses at the whites.

Barbara is no exception. Every whore and pimp and criminal I've ever known or know of has been someone who took the easy way. Not that I don't understand why, or how it's more tempting for the Negro than most whites, or why circumstances make it seem almost impossible to escape at times. I've run against racehorses.

But not as a way of life. And the final difference between all the millions of Negro women, married and single,

who act like women and the handful who are whores is the
difference between every person from the beginning of
time who didn't weaken and those who did. I'm not saying
some people don't have it a helluva lot rougher than others.
But let me tell one thing to these school kids who sit in
antiseptic television studios and preen their Afro hairdos
and spout their dialogues: *no one forces anyone to be a
prostitute.*

Barbara would just love to believe that someone else
did it to her. That's why she demonstrates. Sure, she hates
the white racists. And, to her, all whites are racists. Yet deep
down, hate isn't really what she feels toward them. She
feels need. God, how she needs those whites. Because
underneath it all, the pimp and prostitute and perpetual
welfaree and armed robber are no different from the Uncle
Toms who call themselves militants today.

Without Whitey, there'd be no one to throw off their
own self-hate on. There'd be no one to take the rap for them.

Today's extremists aren't stupid. Usually, they're well
educated, articulate and highly intelligent. But I'm glad
none of my daughters married one. Because no I.Q. is high
enough to break through a mind filled with hate. I've talked
to extremist after extremist in the past six or seven years,
first trying to understand them and later trying to get them
to understand themselves. In every case, I've come to see
how their militancy is in an almost exact proportion to their
lust for revenge and, beneath that, to their own hidden
feelings of self-disgust about themselves.

I've asked them about it. You get all kinds of answers
—cool rationalizations, unconscious coverups, eye-averting
excuses. Once in awhile they'll give it to you straight,
though. One fanatic revolutionary didn't even argue the

point with me about whether or not he wanted revenge. *"They . . . owe . . . us,"* was all he whispered.

I was so struck by his frank hate, I couldn't say anything for a minute. Then I told him, "Yeah, they owe us. You're goddamn right they owe us. But it's a debt we'll never collect on. So why don't you kick the habit?"

He didn't. And he *will* collect. In psychological self-destruction. And in the crippling of a rational rights movement that wants to make sure no new debts are incurred. And even in a possible revolution, but not by militant blacks.

It makes me almost sick to write that last sentence, because what it sounds like is the same old intimidating warning: do this, do that, black man, or Whitey will get mad, and you know what happens when Whitey gets mad. But that's not what I'm saying. I'm saying that blackthink is a vicious, unfair, destructive philosophy and that the massive majority of the people in this country—white *and* black—will never let it flourish even if it means treating looters and rioters like the robbers and arsonists they are.

Yeah, they owe us.

But we're beginning to owe them, too.

7.

I Know Because
I've Been There

"There were people who knew more than others simply because they were more human. It had little to
do with intelligence."

—Dionysus

I know what some of you are thinking: "Jesse Owens can
afford to say all this—he can get away with believing in
Horatio Alger!"

I don't blame you for thinking it, either. Sure, I told
you about my early poverty, I told you about the nightmares I had and about how winning the Olympics turned
out to mean still more poverty and finally bankruptcy.

But I did come out of it. And that my name was Jesse
Owens didn't hurt me any in getting back up. As for poverty
—well, me and a hundred million others. And nightmares?
Who hasn't had them? Some people took their own lives

when Martin was killed. So to many of you my story still might look like a Horatio Alger tale, and my ideas on things the ideas of a fellow who's mainly had it his own way in this world.

It isn't so.

I'm not saying I've had it worse than most, but all in all I haven't had it easier, either. And I'm going to prove that to those of you who consider the source of a man's arguments as important as whether or not those arguments make sense. I'm not going to tell you in detail about the Depression, about living with five other families in a "house" sometimes held together by the number of cardboard boxes you could bring home from the white man's garbage dump (you didn't dare go near his garbage cans). I'm not going to bend your ear with all kinds of tales of government trucks driving into your neighborhood and handing out powdered milk so that the newest baby in the family might possibly live. If you're over forty, you remember it well enough. If you're twenty, it wouldn't mean anything to you anyway.

Nor am I going to tell you about things like the Olympics, though, believe me, it would surprise you if you knew what it took to get there—the sacrifice, the *slaving*. I'm not going to talk about things like that because competition for Olympic victories isn't really what it's all about. There are other, more basic struggles, rougher ones. Every man and woman has them. I'm no different.

First of all, no one would ever even be able to mistake my life for a Horatio Alger yarn if it weren't for some people who kept rescuing me when I was going under for the third time. I've said what my parents did. A lot is expected of parents, but my family went far beyond what was expected of anyone. It was one thing my parents risking a life away from Oakville for the sake of their children, but it was another for them to eat cut-up onions and bread at their two meals a day so I could have the occasional meat in order to run better, and it certainly wasn't expected of my brothers and sisters that they quit grammar or high school and go to work so that I could make college.

No, my family went beyond the call of duty. That's why I couldn't go on to Ohio State until my father had a real job. I appreciate what they did even more now than I did then. I only wish they were alive for me to tell them how much more.

But even with everything my parents tried to do, it wouldn't have been enough for a "success" story without Charles Riley. When he first asked me to go out for the track team in fifth grade, it wasn't because he saw any potential champion in me. It was because he saw a potential corpse. My legs and the rest of me were so thin I looked like a malnutrition case.

But I couldn't run for him. I had jobs every spare minute of the time away from school. And when I was a kid, work was a privilege. "Well, how about before school, then?" he asked me. So every morning three-quarters of an hour before the bell rang, he'd meet me out on the sidewalks by the school and work with me. When I finally broke my first record six years later, he nicknamed me his "sidewalk champion."

Mr. Riley did a lot more than train me to be a runner, though. He brought me food, because he knew I wasn't getting enough at home. And he brought me ideas. He trained me to become a man as well as an athlete.

The funny thing, though, was that he never *told* you

anything. He'd always let you know what he thought by asking the right question or by just saying something that seemed like it had nothing to do with what was actually on his mind. It was so much better that way, because it forced you to think it out yourself so that the answer was really your own.

In the same way, if you ever asked Charles Riley for advice, he'd never answer directly. Instead, he'd tell you a little story and let you figure out the moral for yourself. If you weren't old enough to find it, I guess he figured you weren't old enough to make use of it.

We never talked about white and colored. There was no reason to. He taught *that* by example. His meeting me an hour early in the morning, bringing me food (but always offering it to me honestly, saying, "Here, put some meat on your bones," and not, "The wife cooked this, see how it tastes"), getting my father a permanent job, so many other things—they taught me a lesson I'll never forget even if the blackthinkers line up from here to China shouting it isn't so.

But there were other people who helped me, too. Joe Louis was one. He became the first Negro to win the Associated Press Athlete of the Year Award, in 1935, and I followed in 1936. Not another Negro won it until Willie Mays in the middle fifties, and, until Jackie Robinson came along in 1947, Joe and I had to carry a major load as far as the Negro image was concerned. Of course, there were black men in other fields of endeavor, more than anyone suspects, but sports and show business and politics are what get the attention in this country. There were lots of Negro performers in show business, naturally, but none of them really broke the color line until Nat Cole got a regular TV show in 1957. As for politics, the Negro was lucky to get to vote, let alone run for office in the thirties and forties.

So it was mainly Joe and I. And I thanked the Lord for Joe. Not that I didn't try to live up to the honors I'd been fortunate enough to gain. But big Joe didn't have to try. He was a beautiful, natural man.

In a sense, Joe and I *were* in entertainment and politics as well as athletics. The world was in the grip of the Nazi thing and it was getting worse every day. By knocking out Hitler's Max Schmeling after Joe had taken a beating from him in their first fight, he'd proven once again that free people can get up off the floor and beat anybody. Negro free people, too. Coming after my encounter with Hitler in Berlin, Joe's dramatic first round KO of the Nazi heavyweight really drove home the point.

But above all, Joe Louis drove home another point. If he was a great fighter, he was a greater human being. It came out of his very pores. To watch him walk was to sense it. To just say hello to him was to know it. And almost everyone in this country came to know it. He was the best argument against bigotry the Negro had, even though Joe himself never argued race and wouldn't have had the words to do it if he'd tried.

He did a lot of silly things after he was heavyweight champion, just as yours truly did. He tried to come back with a roll of fat around his middle bigger than a truck tire, he got into big tax trouble with Uncle Sam, he lowered himself to refereeing wrestling matches and almost put one of his ribs through his heart doing it.

But he never hurt anyone outside the ring. In fact, he made a friend of virtually everyone he ever met without even knowing he was doing it. Joe came from patched pants and poverty to make fortunes for dozens of Negroes and a lot of money for thousands of other blacks (though he never put away a dime himself). His name became a household word, in white houses as well as colored. At one of his fights I once heard some white man say to a mink-coated date, "That big dumb nigger might not be able to do another thing, but he sure can fight!"

Joe wasn't dumb, though, and he never—not once—was a nigger, either. He was a constant lesson to me that the knowledge that counts most in this world doesn't only reside in university libraries.

Martin Luther King, Jr., of course, was another person who made a huge difference in my life. I met him before he ever rose to worldwide prominence, and one of the things he showed me better than anyone is that fame can't change a man who's really a man. Someone once said Martin combined the best of Joe Louis and Ralph Bunche. That would make him a human saint. He was. As one writer said, he had the "ability to achieve instant slum clearance by his very presence."

Martin came along at a time when I needed him personally. Life hadn't been any nonstop parade for me after getting on my feet from the bankruptcy. I'd worked hard in the late forties and early fifties, was making ends meet and helping Ruth to raise three daughters, but I still felt I hadn't really found myself. That wasn't easy for a man of forty to admit to himself, but in a way I didn't feel forty. It was as though I'd had two lives, the first ending with the Olympics and riches and then bankruptcy. I'd begun a new life after that, but hadn't really had time to stop and figure out how best to live it. First there were those five years getting out of debt, and then there was another six or eight hustling to do the things for my family I felt I should have done fifteen years before. Oh, the State Department delegated me Ambassador of Sport for the United States in 1955, and in 1956 I went on world tour as personal representative of President Eisenhower in that capacity. It was a real honor, but it didn't make a crucial difference inside.

I traveled around the world and had millions of people wanting to shake my hand again, and when I got home everyone who didn't know would nod his head and smile when he saw me coming, as if to say, "Man, there's the guy who got born with the original silver spoon in his mouth." But in a way Ambassador of Sport was the same old bag, taking me back, not forward, using me for what I'd done, not for what I could do. I was over forty years old, the age when a man is supposed to have built something, and instead all I really had was something that happened nearly twenty years before. Suddenly it wasn't nice having everyone and his brother ask what it was like in 1936—did Hitler really get up and leave when I broke the record, did I get scared when I fouled twice and all the rest. It was a reproach now. I was getting to be just another old jockstrap, as current sports stars refer to former athletes. Maybe I was fur-lined, but I was still a jockstrap.

I had my daughters—great girls—and I had Ruth, though we were knowing our hard times then because she sensed I was hurting inside and wouldn't let me hide from it. The hurt wasn't as dramatic as near-death in Oakville, it wasn't as sharp as finding out you have to ask your parents to sell the house you bought them because you're suddenly bankrupt. But some of the most dramatic things that happen to a man go on within him, quietly, week upon week, until something much more sensational than coughing up blood or being threatened with jail happens. His soul dies.

Martin helped me through that most difficult time. I'm not saying we were the closest of friends. You didn't have to be close to Martin to have him hit you where you lived. Just being a human being was enough for that. I opened up to him one night after he spoke in New York. I didn't mean to. I just meant to discuss civil rights with him for half a minute and let him catch his plane.

But all at once it came out. And it wasn't embarrassing, because you couldn't feel any demeaning emotions when you were with Martin. The hurry to catch his plane vanished. He motioned me aside as if there were all the time in the world, even though the whole thing probably took only a few minutes.

"I think I understand, Jesse," he answered when I was through talking.

Thank god! Someone who didn't say it's all right, not to knock my life because I'd had it so much better than most Negroes, someone who didn't ask me to stop rocking the boat of my own spirit.

"I never knew you that well," he went on. "But I always thought you might have to meet this problem someday. You were like a child prodigy who couldn't go on with what he'd done. And a man must have his work before anything else."

"What *do* I do, Martin?" I said. "It's too late for me to go back to school."

He thought a moment. "All I can tell you is to build on what you know, what you love. You can't run anymore, but isn't there something larger, something related to that part of your life, which you can use as an anchor for the new?"

Then he was gone, on his way to the airport, and I was left alone to catch my own plane in two hours. But what he had said opened up a new way of thought for me. It didn't happen with any flash of light. It took months, years. Yet slowly I began to see that I wouldn't have to cut myself off from my past completely in order to have a future. I did have something to build on. No, it wouldn't be in running the hundred-yard dash anymore, but it could have to do directly with hundred-yard dashes.

I had always loved kids. My own were almost grown, Gloria and Beverly both on the verge of marriage. Part of me had always been a kid at heart myself, maybe a little more than most of us. If I could work with youngsters, help them, mainly through the lesson of athletics, life would truly mean something again. I began looking. In 1955 I was made Sports Specialist dealing with juvenile delinquency for the Illinois Youth Commission, the most gratifying work I'd ever done.

I mainly have Martin to thank for it. Not that he wasn't more human than saint. That's what made him so effective. People knew Martin wasn't putting on. I remember how we were together once watching a TV clip of Malcolm X in his early days. I was studying Martin's face, not the film. Suddenly he noticed.

"What is it, Jesse?" he said.

"I—I thought I saw hate in your face, Martin."

He was silent for a time, as though this was something he really didn't want to admit but had to because he wouldn't be dishonest no matter what the circumstances.

"You did," he said. "Whenever I hear Malcolm and a couple
of others, I begin to hate the white man, too. But just for a
little while, Jesse. It doesn't change anything when I get up
and go out among them."

So Martin wasn't infallible. I think a few of his statements on the Vietnam War were confusing, for instance.
They tended to make some people think that most Negroes
wouldn't want to fight for their country. And I didn't agree
with him at all when he came into Chicago in 1966 and took
over a slum apartment building as if he owned it and col-
lected whatever rents he thought fair. I feel he was frustrated
at the time—his ideals were always so much larger than im-
mediate reality could satisfy—and for one of the few times he
was lashing out in his own way. Not that that anger ever
showed on his face in public. But I knew him well enough
to see that it was there, down inside, and all the greater
because he let it out so seldom.

Most of all, I disagreed with Martin on nonviolence. It
might sound ridiculous to say you idolized Martin Luther
King, Jr. and then say you're against nonviolence, because
that is supposed to be what his movement and ideas were
all about. In one way they were. For Martin was just about
the gentlest, kindest man I've ever known. Yet Joe Louis
made his living as a fighter, and it never changed him. I
think Martin should have fought back more, too. If he
had been prepared to defend himself, others might not have
found him so vulnerable. His great personal gentleness
should have been used to inspire and to shame the violence
out of others. But for those who were too far gone to be
inspired or shamed, I'd have liked to have seen the willing-
ness to fight back backing up that gentleness.

Nonviolence as a way of demonstrating, as a way of

approaching the race crisis legally and ethically through boycotts and then ballots—yes. But I can't see it as a total way of life. It just doesn't work. It didn't for Gandhi in India and, sadly, it didn't for Martin here in America. The black-thinkers with their arsenals of guns laugh at it, as Hitler laughed at the Jews who cowered instead of getting the hell out and organizing against him in some safe place.

There *are* Hitlers. The beautiful thing about Martin is that his very presence on earth reduced them to a minimum. But we will never be without them. Not because men are evil, but because men have an option. And to turn the other cheek when a Hitler or a KKK'er comes and threatens your freedom and your family is wrong. Joe Louis was a counter-puncher. He didn't hit first. But he could hit back.

I loved Martin Luther King, Jr. He was almost young enough to be my son, but he left me with a legacy I can never repay. Yet I wish Martin had had a dozen bodyguards when he stood out on that balcony in Memphis. I think it would have been wiser, kinder to all of us, if that incompara-bly wise, kind man were here today to help this country as he helped me.

There were other people like Martin who contributed to my "Horatio Alger story," too: Bill "Bojangles" Robinson, who offered me a job touring the country with him when I was at low ebb; Ralph Metcalfe, the Phi Beta Kappa become president pro tem of the Chicago City Council who acted like a big brother to me at Ohio State even though we had a fierce competition on the cinders; Larry Snyder, my coach at college, another white man who proved to me again that prejudice is a matter of choice, not coloring.

And more. Most of all Ruth Solomon, the girl I fell in love with at thirteen years of age and don't feel any less for forty-four years later. Ruth helped to pull me through a lot, both as a giggly youngster with a sensitivity far beyond her years and as a mature wife who still owns the spirit of youth.

Not every man may have a Ruth or a Charles Riley, but every Negro has a Martin Luther King and a Joe Louis. If the black man is owed a debt from the past, he owes a debt, too. He owes the men who have come before him, the ones who helped him personally and the many more who helped him by standing up and not copping out when it counted. He owes it to them not to give in to violence and anger, owes it to everyone from Charles Drew, the person who set up the first U.S. blood bank even though his own "black" blood would never be used, to Malcolm X, who finally came from hating all white men to hating only bigotry; from Crispus Attucks, the first man to die for the American Revolution at the Boston Massacre, to Langston Hughes, who always pleaded with his people to simply be eggs before they were colored eggs. He owes it to a lot of men, as yet unborn, who'll stand up in the future in a world that isn't gutted by hatred and rioting.

He owes it to the best in himself.

I've always felt these debts keenly, and maybe that more than anything else is what kept me from cutting a racist's throat with a broken bottle or cutting my own by throwing in with blackthink. Yet even with all the right people behind you, there's more to life than you read in the headlines.

In 1961, I was fired from the Illinois Youth Commission for political reasons. The giant part of my work with the kids I'd been bringing along for six years was over, suddenly cut off like a blade of grass mowed by a power lawnmower.

Losing the Youth Commission work didn't damage me

financially. I'd learned the ways of business through the
years, and my radio show as well as my public relations
agency were flourishing and earning me close to $50,000 a
year. But it was damaging psychologically. I still presented
the same outside to everyone, always ready with a smile and
a burst of energy, but inside was something else. I began to
lose interest in my businesses and allowed them to be run
more and more by associates. Yes, shades of 1939. Slowly
but surely they began taking care of just about everything
for me. When March came, Ruth asked me where the stuff
was to get together our income tax return. I told her some
new fellows I was working with were going to take care of
it. It was the first time in over thirty years of marriage that
Ruth and I hadn't prepared our tax form together.

One March became another and Ruth asked again. I
gave her the same answer. I think she was hurt, but I felt
I had to let these men take over. They were making me
enough money so that I could travel to speak before the
youth groups I needed so much to see. It wasn't quite the
same as working with the kids right on the streets, but it
was close and held me together.

Almost. Giving speeches to the kids finally wasn't quite
enough. As time went on, I hungered more and more for the
real nitty gritty. When I couldn't have it, I tried to get
away from myself, began acting like "the world's fastest
human" again. I got involved in half a dozen other activities,
and, when they weren't going on I was out on the golf course.

One cold winter day in 1965, I got sick. It started as
just a simple cold. I'd had colds before in my life, needless
to say yet I didn't remember ever staying in bed a whole
day with anything for over twenty years. But this one hung
on and went into my chest. On a plane back from New York

one Tuesday night in January I couldn't stop coughing. When I got home, I almost passed out in the elevator. I had dinner and talked with Ruth for about an hour, though most of the time I couldn't speak from the coughing, and then started to change shirts to go down to the station and tape some shows.

Ruth urged me to do it another day. But when you haven't been sick in twenty years, you don't really believe it when it finally happens. I believed it about an hour later. They found me in the elevator at the radio station and rushed me to the hospital. It was double pneumonia, but the doctor loaded me with antibiotics and almost immediately I felt better. By lunchtime the next day I had an appetite like a horse and couldn't wait to get out of the hospital. The doctor advised several days. I left that afternoon.

He gave me some pills to take, but the cough began to get worse again. The following week I was really bothered by it. There was a banquet in Cleveland I'd been looking forward to. I'll just do that one thing, I told myself, and then cancel the rest of the week. It *was* my home town. So I went to Cleveland. On the way back I collapsed again.

This time there was no leaving the hospital early. Both my lungs were filled with fluid, and I was under intensive care night and day. For two nights they had me in an oxygen tent. Finally I came out of it, but I felt weak as a baby and could hardly walk five steps without getting short of breath. They let me go home after eight days, but I didn't play any golf or make any speeches. I just lay in bed reading, watching TV and slowly going crazy. After four days of that, I was looking for any excuse I could find to make it necesary to get out.

I found the best excuse possible. A friend called who

was a key alumnus of a college in California. A change was going to be made within forty-eight hours in the position of athletic director, and he wanted me to fly out and talk to the president of the school the next day. Even though I'd be the first Negro to hold such a job at a white university, he already had a majority committed to me if I could come out and just sew them up.

"Can it wait a week? Even three, four days?" I asked. "Frankly, I want it so bad I can taste it, but I just got out of the hospital with double pneumonia and could use a little more rest."

He was sorry, but it couldn't. So I told him to expect me the next morning. I didn't know what the job paid—probably a third of what I was making—I didn't know when they wanted me to start. I only knew I *had* to have it. When Ruth came home from shopping a half hour later, I was almost packed. I tried to tell her about the call over her protests.

"You're a sick man!" she kept saying. "I know how much this means to you, but there'll be other opportunities."

"No there won't be, Ruth," I said. "That's why I've *got* to go."

I was right. There wouldn't be another opportunity like that one. Yet I didn't get the chance to make good on it. I started coughing blood in the cab to the airport—thank goodness Ruth had made me promise to take a cab instead of drive myself—and by the time we pulled into Midway the driver had to turn around and take me home again. But I didn't see our apartment for three weeks. The next thing I knew I was lying in a hospital bed. They told me I'd been there for five days.

Flashes of those five days jut up from the deep parts of

my memory now and then—my daughters and their husbands standing beside the bed, people in antiseptic gowns putting tubes in my arms, all of it seen through the haze of an oxygen tent. What I never saw was the moment when the doctor took Ruth aside and told her I probably wasn't going to make it. This time the antibiotics weren't working.

She didn't fold up when she heard it. Instead, she gathered up all the strength she had and asked me to gather up what little I had. I vaguely remember her alone in the room with me when everyone else had gone or was sleeping outside, talking to me through the oxygen tent in the moments I was semiconscious, saying, "Fight, Jesse, fight . . . fight. . . ."

I fought. It wasn't much, maybe just a couple of cells inside my brain willing what they could, but I guess it made the difference.

And this time I stayed in bed. The opportunity on the West Coast was gone. But just being alive was something. And I was forming a plan in my mind for when I was better. If a youth job wouldn't come to me, I'd come to it. I'd create it. I was making notes as I'd never done before. I had hit on a way of combining what I'd done for President Eisenhower with the Illinois Youth Commission method I'd worked out, plus what I'd learned speaking before youngsters. It wouldn't just be in the United States, either. What I had in mind would stretch into Canada, South America and India.

First I needed money. I was sure I could get people interested in what I wanted to do once I was able to show them something. But that meant I'd have to start it myself. Though I'd been earning an excellent income for several years, I'd put next to nothing in the bank. It seemed as

though we were always on the brink of saving when something would come along. College for the girls and then their
weddings. Paying my own expenses to speak too often. And
now these hospital bills and the loss of income from being
out of circulation.

It took me almost a month after I got home to do more
than walk around the block. Finally, I went back to business.
I had to make sure things were going right down there if I
was going to save enough to start my international youth
clinics. It had been a long time since I'd been really active
in certain things that were producing income for me. The
man who'd been handling my p-r business was doing fine.
But I knew less about a couple of the fellows who'd more
or less taken over some of my other affairs. A wave of fear
went through me. Could this be 1939 all over again?

I began to look into things, called in an auditor. It was
hard for me not to be the perennial nice guy, but I felt this
once it was necessary. As the days passed, I breathed a sigh
of relief. Things were in good shape, everything was on the
up-and-up.

Only one thing disturbed me. In taking over all these
other things, my income taxes seemed to have been taken
over too. Another April 15 had gone by. The first three
years, I'd asked why they'd never had me even sign my return. "You must've signed it," was the answer. "You sign
so many things, you probably just didn't notice this one."

But how could I have signed it *this* time? I'd been at
home for three and a half weeks and in the hospital for
three more before that. Still, everything had to be all right,
I told myself. If it weren't, I certainly would've heard from
the government by now.

It kept gnawing at me. Ridiculous as it seemed, I had

to make sure my tax returns had actually been filed. Too much was at stake to take a chance, no matter how remote the possibility was. A year and a half from now, I wanted to have enough money in the bank to back me in my project. I'd told Ruth about it and she was excited. For the first time we could really travel together. There'd be some sacrifices, of course, just like in the old days. Now that the kids were gone, we would move to a smaller place as a starter.

It was Saturday morning when the thing came to a head for me. I didn't want to bother anyone on the weekend. Everything else had been O.K., so it wasn't fair to jump on anybody because my imagination might be working overtime. But first thing Monday morning, I decided, I'd check out the taxes once and for all and get that last worry off my mind.

I had a golf date with Ralph Metcalfe and two other buddies. It was the first time I'd been out on the course in months. I'd missed it. Golf had come to mean to me what running had in my youth. I had to have a larger purpose in life than winning gold medals or breaking records, but at the same time I found that I always had to excel in some form of physical competition, too. I'd gotten my game to where I was only a couple of strokes over par, and it provided a rare satisfaction for me. If I get to be ninety—and I doubt very much that I will, because I've lived these fifty-seven so hard—I'll probably be leaning forward in some rocking chair trying to win the old folks' tiddlywinks championship.

I teed up my ball on the first hole and took a few practice swings. "You sure you haven't been sneaking in a few rounds, Jesse?" Ralph kidded me.

I smiled and got ready to hit. I brought my club back in the powerful backswing that had earned me the kidding nickname of "world's strongest human" in our country club. But I didn't bring the club down. I felt a slice of pain like I'd never known. It went through my spine and into my leg. Then just as abruptly as it had come, it stopped.

It stopped because I was numb. I *couldn't* bring the club down, couldn't take a single step. I was paralyzed.

Maybe the thousands of hours of strain on that spine from running and jumping faster and farther than nature meant me to had finally taken its toll. Maybe some germ from the pneumonia had settled in there and destroyed something. I'll never know. I do know that in a single second my life seemed to change more drastically than it ever had before.

I had to be taken from the course on a stretcher. I wouldn't go to the hospital. Once I got home the paralysis let up a little, but the pain started coming back. I couldn't stand or sit, couldn't even find a position to lie in without excruciating agony. Ruth called our doctor and he sent over a specialist. The specialist examined me the best he could. "I'd like to take some X-rays as soon as you can get down to the hospital," he said, "but it looks like a slipped disc. Maybe a ruptured one."

The panic began to leave. I'd known a lot of people with disc problems, athletes in particular. Time usually cured them, though you always had to be careful once you had had them. The days that followed seemed to confirm that. I got better. In a week I was finally able to walk, though bent over some.

I made a date with my associates for noon the following day. I gave myself more than enough time that morning. The hardest part was tying my shoes. I left the house at ten thirty. I was going to drive down myself. I figured I might have to stop a couple of times and stretch out a little. But if driving my car to a business meeting was going to make an invalid out of me, I wanted to know it then and there.

The drive was rough. I had to stop half a dozen times, but getting out and walking around only made it worse. Lying flat on my back in bed seemed like the only way to deal with this. I parked at a lot a couple of blocks from the Sherman, where we were meeting. I wanted to stop off at a currency exchange and cash a check. But I couldn't make it. The whole thing that had happened on the golf course was happening again. I was standing there in the middle of the sidewalk, hardly able to move. Passersby started staring at me, some asking if they could help. A number of people recognized me. "What's wrong, Jesse?" they asked. For a minute, I felt like weeping.

An hour later I was in the hospital again. X-rays with dye were taken. Later that day I got the results. It was a ruptured disc. Maybe I could live with it without going through surgery, the doctor said. Probably not, though. He was a specialist, but he wanted to call in another specialist, the man he thought was the best neurosurgeon in the country, Dr. Eli Tobias.

Dr. Tobias shocked me a little when he first walked into my room the next day. He was so young, and he talked with a British accent. It turned out he was from South Africa. Most of all, he seemed too frail to be a surgeon. He looked to be a couple of inches taller than I was, and yet he couldn't have weighed more than a hundred and sixty pounds. The second time I saw him it would be with his jacket off, and then I would notice the shotputter's forearms he had.

Eli examined me, looked at the X-rays and chatted a little about things in general. Then he rose to leave. "It's really up to you," he said. "These operations are always delicate ones, and your X-rays don't make it look like any cinch. But I do surgery like this three—four days a week sometimes, and I have full confidence that I can handle it. There's always some risk, though, you understand."

I nodded. "What if you *don't* operate?"

"You can try to live with it and see how it goes. My guess is that at best you'd be a little disabled now and then. You'd have to give up athletics and quite a few other things. But it has been done."

"Not *that* way," I said. "I want you to operate as soon as you can. And once you're in there, I want you to do everything—I mean *everything*—that has to be done to make me myself again. I want you to take chances if you have to, even if it means I might not ever get up off that table."

I know that sounds a little dramatic, but I meant every word. I don't like the idea of dying, I don't like it one damned bit. But what I've always been really afraid of is not living as I know I must. As you go on in life, you learn more and more what makes you tick. If you fight it, you destroy yourself. I knew that one of the deep down things for me, one of just a small handful, was *moving*, strange as that might seem. Whether it was running on a Berlin track at twenty-two miles an hour or just walking down Michigan Avenue with spring in my steps, moving my way was part of me. I couldn't give it up, not to age, not to disease.

On May 18, 1965, thirty-six-year-old Dr. Eli Tobias put me under anesthetic for the first time in my life and performed the most delicate kind of surgery on my spine.

Two days later I was standing straight as a javelin, and

nine days after that I was playing golf and making plans
for the future again. That summer I won the championship
of my country club against players half my age, breaking par
in a grueling thirty-six-hole playoff. The trophy I got stands
next to my Olympic medals.

I owe that trophy, and a lot more, to a white African
named Eli Tobias.

I haven't said all this to impress anybody with how hard
I've had it. We've all had sicknesses, and mine were no
worse, no better than those suffered by most men my age.
I do tell you what I have for two reasons. First, so you know
that, all in all, my life is no Hollywood "B" movie script.
But, more important, because it was that siege of sicknesses
that set me up for tax tragedy. And that *was* trouble worse
than most men have had.

It turned out that none of my returns had been filed for
four years.

Before I write another word about this, I want to say
something straight out: the tax thing was my own fault. Yes,
there were situations that led up to it, and circumstances that
helped it to go on for four unbelievable years—unusual situations and circumstances.

But the final responsibility was mine.

I made a damned fool of myself.

Once it happened, my very freedom was at stake. And
second to that, my reputation, the key to whether or not I
earned a living even if I were free. It was the foundation
I'd always had to build on. I'd made mistakes, yes, but not
this kind. It was one thing to go bankrupt because I believed in people to the point of childlike trust. It was another
thing to cheat your government.

I hadn't cheated them. I've never cheated anybody in my life. But I had committed a blunder, and it threatened to cost me everything. The invitations from the church groups and the youth organizations started to dry up like puddles in a sandstorm. What's more, men and women who had been "friends" for years suddenly didn't have time for me. People talked behind Ruth's back at the market. My daughters and sons-in-law were cut day after day by snide remarks from a lot of acquaintances, both white and colored, who seemed to have been waiting for years to see another "idol" smashed down to his feet of clay.

Things were bad for what seemed the longest time. I owed the government a lot of money and had no way of paying it. Above and beyond that, the fine for what I owed could go as high as another $150,000. Of course, there was still another way of paying: going to jail for sixteen years.

Joe Louis had gone through a tax mess, too, and I was one of the people he used to confide in before it ended in 1956. I remember how Joe and I used to sit together during those times. He'd talk about everything but the action against him by Uncle Sam and then, when he couldn't hold it in anymore, he'd let it out and only talk about the tax mess and everything having to do with it.

Except for one thing—going to jail.

Most people are afraid of jail, but I think with some Negroes it's almost an obsession. If you're black you come from a prison. In one sense your whole adult life has been a struggle not to go back. I thought I knew what Joe was going through, especially the one time the big fellow broke down, tears streaming from his eyes, and said, "Jesse, you don't think . . . you don't think they'd . . . put me in *there?*"

But you don't really *know* until you go through it your-self. You live like a zombie, suspended between the past and the future, if there is a future. You insulate yourself against feeling anything because you're afraid you couldn't stand the feelings. Every morning you wake up dreading the thought of seeing people, and each night you go to bed with the next morning standing over you like your executioner. Most of all, as each day sucks more and more from your insides, you have to summon up whatever courage you've got left and struggle against the temptation to not care, to stop fighting and just let them do what they will with you, to give in and simply get it the hell over with.

If my soul didn't cave in, the rest of me started to. I got migraine headaches. I was sick with one flu after another. My stomach started acting up so badly that one doctor diag-nosed it as the sometimes fatal ulcerative colitis. Thank goodness, it wasn't. But I didn't know how much longer I could hold out before something or other did get me.

Then the day came.

My defense wasn't a cop-out. I was guilty of not filing income tax returns for four years. But what I tried to con-vince the judge was that I wasn't guilty of doing it de-liberately. In fact, trying to hurt the country that gave me the chance to accomplish what I had in life was the last thing I'd ever do. Sure, there are injustices within the American system, and they have to be changed. Maybe the tax system is one of them. But I have always believed in changing things from the inside and not going outside with a hatchet. Because the system itself is the freest one that has ever been made by men on this earth.

My lawyer tried to show that to the judge. The U.S. attorney told the other side of the story. Finally, it was time for the judge to decide. I stood up, and he said, "The defendant having been given an opportunity, it becomes the Court's obligation now to pass." It was a little different from being on the Olympic dais, I'll tell you.

"I will not keep you in suspense," the judge began. "I do not propose to impose any extreme penalty upon you."

I felt as though I could have jumped a hundred feet when he said those words. Then he went on: "I do have a few things to say that I think it is appropriate that I might say. . . . The Court has considered all of the testimony that has been presented. . . . You have been subject to tremendous pressure to make personal appearances, to devote yourself to good causes. From my record here, you have been too generous. That has been part of your trouble in your finances. You have been too generous. If I may say so, sometimes it appears to me that maybe you should have had a manager. You have not been selfish enough, probably, to accumulate funds. I have looked at your return here and for the money that you have made, you are not a man of means. I can see where it has gone. It has not gone to riotous living or been thrown away. It has gone to good purposes. . . . I find from my report here and the evidence, that your errors have been errors of omission rather than commission. I find you have been negligent and I am not going to try to excuse you for it. You know it. You have said so now yourself. You have attempted too much. . . . I am convinced that you will never need any more punishment, because you have suffered far more than John Doe, a man on the street, because you have cherished your reputation. Now you have had so much publicity upon it. . . . Never has a defendant stood before the court but what I have taken a look at his record. I hope when I get up above, if I get there and old St. Peter looks down and finds some of my misdoings, I hope at least he will look over at the other side of the ledger and see if there isn't something on the credit side.

"I have looked on the credit side of *your* record here and I see *plenty*.

"Now, having looked at your record and finding that it is good, very good—you have been a good influence—I do not believe there is any reason why this one error should prevent your going right ahead, especially with the attitude in which you approach it here—going right ahead with your good work and keeping it up. I am not going to be the one to stand in the way. . . . While you have been going around . . . supporting our country and our way of life and our democracy, there are other people running around over this country . . . aiding and abetting the enemy openly. It would be a travesty, to my way of thinking, if I under these circumstances exercised my discretion improperly or excessively here against a good citizen for one mistake. . . .

"So I am going to fine you. You are hereby fined $750 for each of the four years, a total of $3,000.

"I am not going to place you on probation, because you do not need probation. You will pay your responsibility, without having to have a probation club over your head. They have got plenty to do to straighten out people rather than to spend their time with *you*. I am convinced if you have got the money, you will pay. . . .

"That is the judgment of this Court."

The judge had talked for almost forty minutes. Now he was through, and it was up to the lawyers and me merely to say, "Thank you, your honor." But I couldn't get the words out. I was too thankful. Judge J. Sam Perry had taught me something that cold February 1 in 1966, something that brought back a line from the movie *High Noon* to me. It was when Marshal Gary Cooper, who, alone, will have to face four killers at noon, goes for help to the last possible man in the town, the former marshal who got him the job and had inspired him all his life. But Cooper's idol tells him what all the rest have: not to fight, to get out, that it isn't worth dying on a dirty street for a bunch of people who don't care.

"It's all for nothin'," he says. "It's all for nothin'."

But it *wasn't* all for nothing.

Of course, I did still owe over $100,000, what with lawyers' fees and everything. I worked as I never had before, even when I was training for the Olympics. I got my six and a half hours a night, but otherwise I went like there was no tomorrow. If somebody wanted me to speak for fifty dollars, I'd fly fifteen hundred miles to do it as long as they'd pay the expenses. What did it matter? I was free— free to work and to pay my debts. And, once they were paid, I'd be free to build my youth clinics all over the world.

It's working out that way, too. My dream is just in the beginning stage, but I think it's a dream that is going to come true. I paid what I owed, dollar by dollar and, as the debt went down, what I thought I'd lost started to grow back. The organizations that had canceled me out began writing and calling again. The Boy Scouts came back first. Then the colleges. And last of all, the National Conference of Christians and Jews. My minimum speaking fee grew to five hundred dollars, and soon I was one of the ten current sports stars in greatest demand, even though I hadn't competed in almost two generations.

As of right now, I've been to twenty countries in the

last four years, and I've planned double that for the next four. Yet even if something should happen to me, even if I checked out tomorrow and never got to see my idea grow into what it can be, I can't complain. But I sure don't know who Horatio Alger is. Because the battles that count aren't the ones for gold medals. The struggles within yourself—the invisible, inevitable battles inside all of us—that's where it's at.

Life is the *real* Olympics.

8.

Showcase the Good

"Say, hey!"—Willie Mays

It's Friday night in Detroit. A gang of half a dozen colored teen-agers are roaming the streets, looking for trouble. A year ago, maybe less, they'd gone out on those streets at night only as petty thieves or pranksters. Yet somewhere in the months that followed, they turned into criminals. Pills made them looser, booze made them bolder. Eventually they traded dime-store pilfering for armed robbery and assault.

Of course, that's no big event in most Negro neighborhoods. What these four fifteen-year-olds and two fourteen-year-olds will do tonight is an "event" in any neighborhood, though. They'll get wild on speed, enter an apartment and make a man watch while they rape his wife and eleven-year-old daughter. Then they'll take all the money in the house and beat everyone senseless to erase the memories for them. . . .

It's Saturday night in Fort Worth, Texas. A Negro man has just gotten off work and is walking home. He stops to look in a store window. Two cops cruising in a squad car pull up. The crime of the night before—and the near riot of the week before—has made *them* bolder, too. They climb out and ask the fellow what he's doing. He tells them, but nervously. But he's telling them only a block and a half from where the crime took place. They arrest him. . . .

In Waukegan, Illinois, there's a slum. The people living in it are existing in the worst kind of filth. Their stairways and elevators are filled with feces. The halls smell like urinals. The electric dishwashers are filled with garbage and the garbage disposals are broken.

Yet few people on the outside know that this is a ghetto. They know that the project was built so that people from the Chicago and Waukegan and even Gary area could come and have a better life, and they think this is just what's happened. Because on the outside, the project is still beautiful.

It isn't unique. There are projects like it from one end of the country to the other. . . .

Hal and Lara Sue live in an apartment in San Francisco. They have two children, Randy, seven, and Phyliss Sue, three. They love each other, have never flirted with another man or woman, let alone had any affairs during the nine years of their marriage. They're both in good health, and Hal has an excellent job, making $17,000 a year with bright prospects of much more. He's never been in jail, and neither one of them smoke pot or drink too much. Both have a college education. And despite it all, the world won't let them live. Because Hal is black and Lara Sue is white, and most people won't let them forget it for a single minute. . . .

In New York, it's a new school day. Only in one huge area, hardly any kids are going. Their parents are keeping them home. Why? Because they've become convinced that their children should be taught only by black teachers.

Yet there are no black teachers, or at least not anywhere near enough to handle all the Negroes in New York City, to say nothing of the rest of the country. Most school boards have tried to hire every single black instructor they could find, have even bent requirements to let in any Negro who's even half qualified. But you can't change three hundred years of history in one semester. There just aren't that many black teachers. Yet as long as their kids are taught by whites, a lot of people in New York City and hundreds of other places will prevent kids from getting any real education at all and may sometimes disrupt an entire school system. . . .

In St. Louis, there's a thirty-year-old woman on welfare. Even though she's never been married, she has four children and is going to have as many more as she can as long as it means extra money from the government. Janet has almost no feeling for these children, and much of the time they're left uncared for with only a neighbor from across the hall to hopefully look in on them now and then. Cut off Janet's money, and you cut off money to a lot of other women who're genuinely trying. Keep sending the checks and you throw her check and thousands of others down a rathole. . . .

It goes without saying that these are all complex prob-lems, any one worth a book in itself. Also, needless to say, there are people much more expert than Jesse Owens at most all of them, people who've devoted their lives to solving just one facet of the "race situation" in America.

So I'm certainly not going to presume to give final answers. What I feel I can do is to draw on my experience to indicate some directions that might be taken with certain fundamental kinds of dilemmas. My experience hasn't been only as a Negro who's known both up and down, but as someone who's worked for local, state and federal systems—and worked to change those systems as a private citizen.

So where do you start?

Though one of the mistakes made today by both moderates and militants in my opinion is that they hardly ever go behind the symptoms of the crisis to its real root, I still think you have to begin with the violence that seems to be erupting all over. Though it stems from far less than a single percent of the people in this country, the violence is disturbing and must be reckoned with.

But before you do anything, I think you have to recognize that there are two kinds of violence. The serious and involved student who is rightfully boycotting a restaurant and pushes back when someone wrongfully pushes him, for example, is a world apart from the loaded-for-bear militant who is there mainly to make sure someone gets pushed. The kids who demonstrated in Chicago at the Democratic National Convention two years ago were mostly an idealistic breed who only wanted to express themselves freely, and a far cry from some of the professional agitators who set off Newark or Cleveland. Now a policeman or a politician may not be able to tell one from the other, but there are people—from concerned citizens to professors and students themselves—who can. They should be brought in to help.

For I feel the law has been used doubly indiscriminately

where violence is concerned. Kids should not be arrested for hitting back. No one should. Defending yourself against the Establishment is only against the law in Communist and fascist countries, not here. People marching in peaceful demonstrations, whether it's in front of the White House or on a southern dirt road, should be protected to the limit *by* the police *against* those who don't understand what it is to protest for something you believe in.

By the same token, anyone who uses violence to get his way, whether it's by throwing a rock or robbing a gas station, is a criminal and should be dealt with as a criminal. I'm not arguing that the criminal isn't sick and that you shouldn't go to society at large and find the causes of his illness before you can effectively reduce violence in the United States. But while you're avidly searching for those causes, you have to go on living. That means that criminals must be punished. They can be rehabilitated once they're sentenced, but their sentences must be fair—not only for them, but for those they attacked. I'm against vindictive punishment. I don't think severe punishment as a deterrent against further crime necessarily works. But I also believe in a just society. And when you punish someone who is using violence, the *first* consideration has to be the protection of those he used the violence against and of those others against whom he might use it in the future. That rapists can go back out on the streets in two years and attack the same woman is even worse than keeping them locked up for a lot longer without attempts at rehabilitation, though neither is good. There must be a third alternative.

Just because society has produced criminals doesn't mean that everyone in America is sick and shouldn't have the right to live out his life in his way, free of rapists and riots, muggings and militants. There are a lot of decent people around. Oh, they can almost all be improved. But not by seeing fire set to their businesses or living under the threat of having their heads blown off.

I think there will probably have to be a reorientation of the forces of law and order in this country for what I want to come about. Most policemen do what they're told, are only supposed to see the surface of things, and not be psychoanalysts or sociologists. But if the guidelines for law enforcement are changed—to be both stricter *and* more lenient, as the situation demands—police behavior will change and eventually there won't be the riots or the crime in general that there is today.

That has to start from high up. J. Edgar Hoover has said many times that the first goal of our society is law and order and that this distinguishes us from other countries. President Nixon says Hoover has his full confidence. Well, he doesn't have mine, because I feel the first goal of our society is *justice—freedom*. Law is only the means to those ends, order only the result of using laws the right way to achieve the ends. When you start to get widespread disorder, that isn't a signal for stricter laws and more arrests. It's a sign that some of the laws you already have or some of the people enforcing them are unjust.

Yet the responsibility for a less violent society goes far beyond the enforcers of the law. It radiates back and forth between the heartbeat of the man on the street and his leaders in every segment of society. I like many of President Nixon's economic policies, because I've learned from my own life that you can't spend more than you've got, but I'm disturbed at some of his larger ideas on law and order, too. He's for wiretapping and legally controlling obscenity, for instance. Now I don't like pornography. But you won't control it by passing laws and having policemen arrest the people who don't obey those laws. Sometimes it seems as though the Democrats are always trying to confiscate your bankbook and the Republicans are continually trying to take away your library books. *Someone* should have learned from Prohibition.

Education is another thorny problem, partly because it will take a generation to get the black teachers needed. The books themselves are changing, though. Publisher after publisher, easily a majority by now, are putting Negro history into textbooks as fast as it can be written. Frankly, I think the trend is well underway here and that many federal, state and local school boards are doing a lot. Others, especially in the South, should be pressed to join them. But what must be accomplished—and what can only be accomplished by going to the root of the black/white problem—is for the Negro to become convinced that it's most important for him to get an education, regardless of who he gets it from. One of the most disturbing things about blackthink is its new anti-intellectualism, its rejection of learning simply because that has been the white man's bag. I'm no intellectual, but I'm damned sure that if the Negro wants to fulfill himself, he'd better make certain he fills up on learning.

Housing and welfare obviously aren't simple issues, either. So much of the money for these has been like the foreign aid we've given to dictatorships. It never reaches the people and, when it does, it ends up buying the same kind of lives for them, only with a little better facade. But what are you going to do with the women who have five kids and genuinely can't feed them? And are you going to leave the slums as is? Here I think President Nixon has shown wisdom in saying that the federal government has

gone about as far as it can go. For the Negro who hasn't
yet made it isn't going to make it through welfare money
or an apartment in a modern housing project. He needs to
build his own house. But I don't think "black capitalism"
is the answer. I think we'll need some "gray capitalism"—
a mixture of black and white. And that goes back to the
root of the problem again.

For nothing goes to the heart of the race crisis more
than the *social* crisis between black and white today. Just
about everything starts there, and that's what we've got to
recognize. If the black welfare mother resents the white
social worker who O.K.'s the check, that check is buying
hate. If the suburban white with her colored maid never
exposes her kids to any other Negroes, she's hiring more
than a maid. She's hiring ignorance. How can Hal and
Lara Sue and their kids get along in this world if no Negro
feels he can get along in Richard Nixon's Cabinet or if my
next-door neighbor and I feel we can't get along with each
other?

And what about jobs, not in the White House, but for
the lowest laborer? In 1967, *Newsweek* said: "Improving
a man's living conditions won't help him much unless he
has a job. A job won't help him unless he is trained to
perform it. He cannot be trained without the conviction that
he has a chance to succeed." So we always come back to
blackthink and its deadliest poison: though it converts almost no one, it silently brainwashes many Negroes to deny
everything they can see with their own eyes and thus deny
themselves the benefits that are now theirs for the taking.

What can be done about it—and everything else?

Three basic things, I think.

First, you *work long range*. Don't expect to undo hundreds of years in a month or two. Or a year or two. Most of us agree pretty much on the seed of today's race crisis —the one tyrannical decision the United States made when it broke away from Britain's tyranny: to keep some human beings less than human by calling them slaves.

The rules that existed for all those years of slavery still haven't been broken down a hundred percent, socially and mentally. Until *you*, white man, can see *me* walk into a restaurant and not stare any more than you would if another white walked in, the house of prejudice still stands. And until *you*, black man, can walk into that restaurant and not expect to see stares—and not care if you do—you're still sharecropping.

I said that Charles Riley never gave advice. But there was one exception to that, something he said so often that you didn't even think of it as advice: "Train for four years from next Friday." He first told it to me when I was a runty grammar school kid who'd just been convinced by him to come out for the track team and who wanted to quit because my legs looked like pieces of straw next to the other guys'.

"I'll never make it this year, Mr. Riley," I said to him dejectedly.

"Who says we're trying to make it *this* year?" he answered. "You're training for four years from next Friday, Jesse."

Without the pressure of having to change overnight from a sickly specimen to an athlete, I learned to enjoy running, and that was one reason for my developing the "picture form" people said I had. I was relaxed out there on the track, mentally and physically, and I think the same goes for anybody trying to get anything done.

But there were days when the pressure would mount. It was fine in high school when I started breaking records, except the time soon came when I couldn't improve on my past performances and even dropped down a bit. I was like the show business star who has nothing left for an encore, who's afraid of today because of yesterday's success.

"Where do I go from here?" I finally asked Mr. Riley.

"Keep training," he'd answer.

"For what?"

"Why, for four years from Friday, of course."

I took his advice. Four years from Friday turned out to be the Olympics.

After Berlin, though, there really *was* nothing left as far as running was concerned. When the bad months began to add up and the personal depressions overtook me more and more, I often thought of going back to Charles Riley for advice. But I knew what he'd say. Train for four years from next Friday. It wasn't easy to keep that in the front of my mind, but I did the best I could and it did help to steer me toward finishing college. Afterward, it gave me the heart to work through fourteen hundred days and nights to pay off the huge debt I'd been saddled with.

I didn't follow that advice because Good Man Charles Riley said it. I followed it because it worked. And that's one of the key things that is so wrong with blackthink. It doesn't work, because it's short range. It's, "Do it all now or forget it!"

Well, you can't do it all now. A movement has to grow like a tree or, better still, like a man. It has to go through the seasons, sometimes without water and sometimes in the burning sun until, an inch at a time, it reaches to the sky.

But being long range doesn't mean you can't be totally

involved. A movement has to care, and care down to the inside of its bones about today's injustices, just like a man has to *want* to grow, *here, now.* Having a perspective doesn't mean you have to lose the *now.*

Yet approaching the crisis in this way is only a first step. The second step is to *understand the nature of the crisis itself.* And the truth that almost everyone, white and black, keeps forgetting is that this is *not* now fundamentally a problem of race. It's a problem of *people.*

For every bit of bigotry against blacks, there is prejudice against yellow skin, against Jews, sometimes even against white Protestants. For every poverty-stricken Negro, you can find two poverty-stricken whites. There are proportionately more Negroes in trouble than whites, but a white man's empty stomach acts the same as a black man's, and a white woman gets just as terrified when a black intruder enters her home as a black woman does when a white man enters hers.

Violence, poverty, prejudice, all the rest—these aren't Negro problems. These are *people's* problems. Someone would have to be blind not to see the unrest of the entire younger generation going on all around us. And you'd have to be deaf not to hear why they're restless. For the "Negro problem," like everything from Vietnam to pollution, is only a *symptom* of the real crisis of our times, not the crisis itself. Until we realize this, I honestly can't see how we're going to solve either the race problem or the bigger one that lies beneath it—the problem of a world that seems to be going to hell.

I don't think most of today's draft card burners would have minded fighting Hitler. But even our own leaders aren't agreed on why we've let more than a quarter of a

million lives be maimed or lost in Vietnam and spent longer
there than in any war in our history. First we hand a world
like that down to new generations, and then we ask them to
go off and die for it while we sit and press the buttons—
the wrong buttons.

Not that I think the world *is* going to hell. But I do
feel history will show that this was mankind's turning
point, the time when everything got fearfully complicated
and when, for America, all our big mistakes came back at
once to haunt us. Yet I also feel that if the younger generations weren't deeply disturbed about it all, we *would* be in
trouble. I'd like to see more people my age as involved as
their kids. Too many of my own generation act like hippies
without the beads. They've turned off and dropped out just
as much as the pot smokers in Haight-Ashbury. "What can
I do?" a man I've known for years asked me the other day.
"I mean, how many years have I got left, Jesse?"

"Man," I told him, "that's the point. I ask myself how
many years I've got left and that's what makes me want
to get these things done."

I'm not asking this man to spend that much time
working to change this world. As I've said so many times,
the man I respect most is the one who quietly does his
thing in his way.

But you do live in the world, so it's sometimes part
of your thing. To *ignore* what's happening around you isn't
a mark of maturity. Doing your thing in your way sometimes does mean getting involved. Above all, it means first
giving some thought to things. Because a man's daily attitude in the thousand and one situations he comes up against
is more influential in society than his joining this committee
or that.

And no matter what one does, *the good must be show-cased.*

Everyone today is almost exclusively concerned with correcting what's wrong with America. Some of that *has* to be done. But we act as though that's all there is. And it's precisely because of this that we're all so hung up on the negatives. The result is that two gigantic truths have begun to escape us.

The first is that there's a lot more good than bad going on. If there weren't, you *would* have a revolution. If there weren't, *you*—whether you're black or white, young or old, rich or poor, moderate or militant—wouldn't be reading my words.

Second, no matter how much bad there is, the very best way to get rid of it is *by exposing the good*. Don't just hack away at the roots of evil. They go all the way to China. Plant next to prejudice another tree that grows so big and high that discrimination has to wither and die.

Those aren't just words, either. They're a code of action. One thing they mean is that it's more important for a Negro golfer to play in the Masters than it is for a hundred Negro athletes to give nationwide speeches telling how they'd correct injustice.

For there are too many times when the good hasn't been showcased. I remember one incident a few years ago. Arthur Ashe, Jr., the Negro tennis champion, was scheduled to play an exhibition in Chicago's West Side Armory for some ghetto kids who'd reluctantly come off the streets to join a tennis program run by business executive and former tennis star Grant Golden. I know those kids and, though they wouldn't have admitted it to you in so many words, this was the biggest event in their lives. For weeks their schools had been plastered with posters saying that Ashe was coming all the way from wherever just to play a match for *them* in the midst of their squalor.

For these grade-school youngsters, this was the American dream coming true—twice over. First, Arthur had proved that it could be done. His father started as a janitor, and yet Arthur had become the best in this country at something, and the best in the most lily-white sport around. Second, he was coming to see *them*. He was saying, "I care about *you*." And if Arthur Ashe cared about them, how could they fail to do a bit of what he'd done in this world?

People talk about all the evil influences on a ghetto Negro, and there are a lot. They pile up day by day, threatening to snap a soul, twist a mind. But let me tell you something. One dream come true, one glimpse of the world as it can be, is all that it takes to dissolve that nightmare.

They said only seventy-five kids could fit into the armory that cold December day. But the place was busting with twice that many. Everybody—even the twelve- and thirteen-year-olds who were beginning to harden toward the world—wanted to see Arthur. Some of the parents had taken off from work to be there.

Arthur Ashe, Jr. is one of the kinder athletes I've met and is pretty mature for a young fellow who's had so much fame thrust upon him so young. But without really knowing it, he made a mistake that day. He let Sargent Shriver convince him to accept some award somewhere and do an interview in a national magazine about what he thought could be done to remedy society's ills, instead of coming to Chicago and playing tennis for a handful of ghetto kids.

Until he reads this, he probably won't even have realized that the millions of whites and Negroes who read his words in that magazine weren't a pimple on the behind of what it would have meant to those hundred plus grammar school youngsters to see *the* Arthur Ashe walk into their bailiwick and hit a few tennis balls. I'm not picking on Ashe. It's *because* he's an outstanding guy that I use him as an example. For, like almost everyone else today, Arthur doesn't fully realize how real progress is made in this world. It's made the same way with other people that you make it in tennis. One shot at a time. One kid at a time. But, oh, how that one slice of bread sails out on the waters of mankind—just a single tough kid going back to school the next day, his attitude slightly changed because he's *seen* it, it's happened to *him,* and all the widening circles in the waters of his acquaintances that this slightly changed attitude touches, and then all the tidal waves of influence that *those* kids produce when they finally go out into the world.

Rod Laver, the number one tennis player in the world, replaced Arthur that day. He didn't mean shit to a hundred ghetto grammar schoolers.

They sat in the stands and watched as though they were numb. A couple had trouble holding back the tears. But the others were too tough for that. And after that day, they were tougher. We'll hear from some of them, believe me. When it's too late for them to be changed by awards to their former heroes or any high-sounding interviews in national magazines.

As I said, I'm not knocking Arthur Ashe. I use him as an example *because* he's a fine young man. The mistake he made is no different from the mistake everyone is making. But it's still a crucial one.

People, Negroes in particular, have criticized Willie

Mays, for example, because he didn't get involved politically or march on the streets like some of our other sports or entertainment figures. They don't know how many hospitals Willie has quietly visited, how many crippled or critically ill kids he's promised they'd play ball again.

But if he'd never even signed a single autograph for a youngster, Willie Mays would still have done more for the Negro than most of his "involved" peers put together. Every time he went back for a drive he couldn't possibly catch, and caught it, every time he doubled off the wall when they were throwing him low and outside in a clutch situation, every colored kid in America—and a lot of white ones—knew for sure even if they never thought about it that life was worth living and that this world was, all in all, a pretty good place. He didn't have to prove he was involved. Willie Mays was as involved in what he did as any man I've ever seen. And he didn't have to tell any kids he cared about them, either. He showed something more important—that he cared about *life,* and cared to the hilt. *That's* what they want to know—that a Negro can feel THAT.

I learned the same thing in the midst of the Depression from watching Babe Ruth and reading the life of George Washington Carver.

Sound too simple?

Try it.

Find the good. It's all around you. Find it, showcase it and you'll start believing in it. And so will most of the people who come into contact with you.

Showcase the good.

Believe in it.

It's real, baby.

9.

Black Man,
Heal Thyself

"There are many ways to call yourself a nigger."
                                        —*Dionysus*

Some of my best friends are Negroes. But not all.

Though everybody seemed to know us when Ruth and the girls and I came to Chicago to live in 1949, hardly anybody was really close to us.

My Olympic experiences had preceded me, but my relatives and our good friends were still in Cleveland and Detroit. Ralph Metcalfe was in Chicago but awfully busy, Joe Louis was only in and out and for the most part it was a cool town even if people were always coming up and asking for my autograph or wanting me to speak somewhere.

But pretty soon we made some new acquaintances.

We found ourselves playing cards with three other couples now and then. I'm not much of a card player, but I went along. I couldn't go to many sessions, because I was traveling to speaking engagements. But I made those I could so that Ruth could have a little something to replace what we'd known back home.

Once or twice it struck me that the three men and their wives were all rather light-skinned. Ruth and I both happen to be the same. But I didn't give it much thought.

A Friday arrived when it was our turn to give the party, and one couple couldn't come at the last moment because the fellow came down with a virus. "Don't worry—I'll find someone else," Ruth told the wife. "We've got some next-door neighbors here who are just lovely."

"Er . . . Ruth, why don't you call one of the other girls. Maybe they'll know someone," she answered.

But Ruth invited our neighbors, and the evening, though it lasted only an hour and a half, was a long series of excuses. One of the wives suddenly developed a bad headache. After she and her husband left, I suggested threesomes. But our other regular couple couldn't, they said. They'd forgotten that they had to be up early tomorrow to drive to Wisconsin.

After they left, I went back into the living room and sat down. "Jimmy and Alyce say they have to leave, too, Jesse," Ruth told me.

"Wait a minute," I said. "Will somebody please tell me what's going on here?"

There was a nervous silence. Jim came up to me. "Jess," he said quietly, "we've already ruined your evening with your friends. I think it's best that we don't stay and louse it up any further."

"What are you talking about? How did you ruin it?"

He stammered. "Don't you really know?" Alyce said.

I shook my head. "Is there bad blood between you and—"

"Not bad blood," she shot back. "Bad *skin*. We're *dark*, you see. And they just don't associate with any dark-skinned Negroes."

We didn't see our other "friends" again. It was a shock when I heard the truth, but thinking back I could see how it was. Not that this was the first time I'd ever encountered Negroes who were prejudiced against Negroes because their skin was dark. It happened in my boyhood in Cleveland, it happened in my fraternity house at Ohio State, it's happened hundreds and hundreds of times since.

I remember when one of my daughters was dating a very good-looking light-skinned young fellow in college. Honor student, three-sport man, all the rest. She liked him too, until he started asking about what color her grandparents were. He was thinking of marriage, you see, and wanted to make sure none of the children came out dark brown or black.

They didn't get married.

Negroes often used to tell the story of the colored boy skipping down the street after school and dreaming how wonderful it would be to be white. "If I'd be white, everything'd be right," he's singing. He skips by a wooden fence that is being painted and suddenly a bucket of white paint falls on him from above. He wipes his eyes and looks at himself. He's white all over!

As fast as he can the boy runs home. "Look, Ma!" he shouts happily. "I'm white!"

His mother shrieks, "Go to the bathroom and clean off that stuff!"

He's undaunted and rushes into the bedroom. "Look, Sally! Look, Marna!" he yells to his older sisters. "I'm white! I'm white!"

"Don't get any of that stuff on me!" one of them screams. "Get out of my room, and don't you touch anything until you get clean!" the other says.

He decides to hole up until his father comes home. His father will understand. He goes off to the basement until he hears the head of the house coming in the front door. Then he rushes upstairs and yells, "Dad! Dad! Look at me! Isn't it wonderful? I'm white!"

His father looks at him. "Don't sit down to the dinner table until every spot of that is washed off," he says firmly.

Dejected, the boy goes into the bathroom and starts to fill the tub. "Damn," he mutters to himself. "I've been white a half hour and already I hate those black bastards!"

I said in the first chapter of this book that the dream of being white haunted me through my youth as it haunts every Negro. But that doesn't mean that if the chips were down and a real choice had to be made, a majority of Negroes would actually change the color of their skins. Being white is more a fantasy, like being Howard Hughes, or being marooned on a desert island with a harem of beauties, or living forever. Every man is haunted by these thoughts occasionally, and the Negro doesn't need to feel guilty about them unless he really comes to hate his black skin so consciously and purposefully that his whole life becomes altered by this hate.

Unfortunately, there are a number of Negroes who go that route. Some aren't as obvious as those three couples we played cards with, but the prejudice is there just the same. Too many blacks love their own "whiteys." If they happen to be dark, they tag after the light-skinned Negro as an ugly girl latches onto a pretty one. If they were born light, they use it as a status symbol, something that puts them in a safe limbo somewhere between the black and white man.

Historians say this started in slave days when the plantation bosses got to like some of the mulatto children who were produced when they took the Negro women from the slave quarters for a night. Also, a light Negro could pass up North and say he was Spanish or something. But I don't think you have to go back that far. Let's face it: for a long time, white *has* seemed "right," and if you were black, you *did* have to get back. The hair straightening and the popularity of the Caucasian-looking Lena Horne types prove the point.

That some of us still love our own "whiteys," that *we* are prejudiced against Negroes, has long been a taboo subject among black people—above all when they're talking to whites. But we've got to come out with it, and then deal with it, because until Negroes can rid themselves of prejudice against Negroes, how in the hell can they expect whites to act fair?

The blackthinkers are the worst offenders of all. Their recent craze toward Afro-dress and hair styles is just a final ironic sign that down deep the militants are more insecure about their skin color than anyone. They make too damn much of it, protest far too much about how nice it is. They're like the guy who's always talking about how great he is in bed. If something's that good, you don't talk about it. Joe Louis never told anybody he was strong. Martin never had to say, "I'm a gentle man."

Ira is tall, broad-shouldered and the kind of fellow you figure might have been a professional athlete ten years ago. He *was* a football star in a Chicago high school but never could stay interested in athletics as a career because of what had to be put out physically. He did get interested in women and, by the time he was seventeen, found he could live nicely by playing the gigolo. He'd pay some of the Negro women who worked as maids in white homes to let him pick them up at work, saying he was their brother. In this way he was able to meet susceptible rich white females. One time a woman hired him not for herself, but for her husband, who was homosexual. Ira went along.

In his late twenties, he was making from seven hundred to a thousand dollars a week. Ira had access to two new Cadillacs whenever he wanted. There were open charge accounts for him at three plush haberdasheries. He didn't move out of the ghetto, though. Instead, he got himself a big apartment right smack in the middle of it and fixed it up like one no one had ever seen. The most expensive furniture, built-in stereo and closets full of smart clothes.

Today Ira stays in the ghetto because he has to. He doesn't have any nine-room apartment anymore, and most of his fine furniture has been sold off. His income is mainly unemployment checks and an occasional ten- or twenty-dollar fee he can get for a one-night stand with some woman who isn't too choosy. Usually, her paying for the dinner and drinks is all he gets. Ira is almost forty now, has lost that boyish appeal, that certain class, that hard-to-define magnetism he once had as a young man. He drinks too much and often wears the same sport coat two nights in a row, something he never would have done a few years ago.

But even if Ira should somehow walk into a thousand

a week again, he'd never leave the ghetto. Just as he didn't leave it a decade ago. It's *home* to Ira. No matter how much money he makes, he'll always come back to the ghetto's level. For Ira himself, not the dilapidated buildings or the crud in the halls or any circle on a city map, *is* the ghetto.

So is Harold. He's no gigolo, no alcoholic, no dope addict. As a matter of fact, he works at a regular job five days a week, though he doesn't work overly hard. His health is only fair. His children are grown and his wife is separated from him. He feels the need for a family life, for a woman, but he never gets around to doing anything about it. He's tired when he comes home and usually flops down in the big chair with the stuffing coming out of it in front of a twenty-one-inch color TV, a six-pack of beer beside him, and watches until he dozes off after Johnny Carson or the late movie.

Harold is fifty-three now. Once he was young, a high school graduate with a good future in front of him. Maybe he'd go to college. Maybe he'd take a year in Europe. Once he was twenty-five with a pretty new wife, who wanted him to go back to school nights while she worked so he could move into a better field and they could live in a classy mixed part of Birmingham. She'd dreamed of it her whole life.

Harold thought it would be nice to move there, too. Only he never got around to going to school, and after Sheila became pregnant with their first child, he couldn't afford school without the second pay check coming in. Still, twenty years ago he was a man of thirty-three with two fine little girls and a wife who seemed better educated than most of the women in the neighborhood. Sheila never read those true confession magazines. She read *Time* and even *Harper's*.

Sheila lived with Harold until the girls married, and then she left. She didn't want to see the whole dream die. So now Harold lives by himself in a little two-room flat right off one of the worst sections in Birmingham. Three years ago last July he got mugged while walking into his apartment, and his health has never been the same since. He sees double sometimes and once or twice has passed out at work. But he won't be doing that much longer. He knows they're going to lay him off one of these days. He cares about it—but not enough. Just as he wanted to move to a new suburb with his wife, he really did want to—but not enough.

There were so many things in this world that Harold wanted if he could have gotten out of the ghetto. But he simply didn't want them badly enough. Going to school at night, holding a second job a couple of evenings a week, these things take effort. Harold wasn't willing to put out that effort. It was easier to come home at night and drink the beer, just as it's easier now. And that's just what the ghetto is to Harold. Not an address. But a way of life. The *easy* way.

Margaret's adored father died when she was only eleven, from an automobile accident with his drunken wife at the wheel. Margaret's mother was jailed only for a few months so she could take care of her daughter. But four years later the daughter left. It would have been sooner, except that Margaret didn't want to leave her younger brother helpless with their alcoholic mother. At fourteen he joined the navy. The same day Margaret walked out on her mother and has never seen her again.

She hasn't walked out on the ghetto, though. She lives there and works there, as a policewoman, apprehending everyone from hardened prostitutes to grammar school costume jewelry pilferers. And she treats them all the same. With cruelty. Even the women she's able to seduce.

For Margaret hates the ghetto and the people in it. Yet she can't leave. She has to stay there, because that's where over and over again she can punish the woman who punished her by killing her father. More than once, Margaret's superiors have had complaints about her. But she does most of her work too efficiently to be reprimanded. And anyway, "you have to be tough on them" in the ghetto. Nine times out of ten, the black cops are harder on their own than the white policemen are. Margaret is even tougher than the male black cops.

Hughie isn't tough at all. He's an addict and he'll do anything on this earth to get himself a fix when he needs it. And yet Hughie stays in the ghetto for the same reason that Margaret does. Revenge. This is his form of black-think. By being completely dependent on society, by becoming a total parasite, he is actually lashing out at the system. In the only way he can, by being a burden to them, he's punishing those who have made it.

Franklin resents the idea of being a burden to anyone. Twenty-seven, college educated, he lives in the ghetto because he feels no Negro should leave until everyone can. To him, the Iras and Harolds and Margarets and Hughies are all products of the buildings in which they live, not at all the other way around. Franklin is a militant, and he stays out of "pride," just as he flaunts his "African heritage" in every other possible way. His motive for living in one of the worst slums on the eastern seaboard may be exactly opposite to Harold's or Margaret's. But they all have one thing in common.

They could leave if they wanted to.

For Margaret and Franklin, it could be today. For Harold and Ira, maybe a few months. For Hughie, years. Maybe never. But once he had the chance. He had it time and again and he dashed it to pieces.

Hughie didn't only jump. He was pushed. And there are others who, free will or no free will, had what almost amounts to no chance at all of getting away from the rats and the feces-filled halls. But they're in the minority.

You can give long psychological explanations as to why everyone in the ghetto is tempted to stay. The guilt of going when almost everyone you know stays behind. The fear of retaliation if you leave. A dozen other reasons. There's some truth in all of them. But there's more truth in this: just as many Negroes are as prejudiced against black skin as are the worst white racists, so a staggering number of Negroes who live in the worst slums stay there *because they want to.*

Just as whites stay in their slums.

Just as most of us stay in the slums of our souls longer than we ever have to. Sometimes our whole lives.

Yes, some are locked in. Some never have a chance. Some are pathetic victims.

But mostly it's a matter of choice. Those sound like hard words, I know. But there are hard facts to back them up. The most revealing fact is that millions of Negroes have already made the choice.

They've left the ghetto. Or they've turned "the ghetto" into a fit place to live.

On 62nd Street in Chicago, there is a row of houses. There's an almost identical row in hundreds of other towns in this country. It isn't the only street like that in any one of those places, either. There are dozens. They're part of the "ghetto," even though they don't look like it. They usually fringe the really bad slum areas. Often there are six or eight houses, with an apartment building or two at the corner.

They're big houses, many built in preghetto days when there weren't many Negroes in these cities at all. Some of them were rather majestic homes. A few still have that look—on the outside. On the inside, it's something else again.

Salesmen eat up these neighborhoods, but only on a cash-purchase basis. Because if you take an order and come back two weeks later with the merchandise, you stand a good chance of having the family who bought it not living there anymore. The house won't be empty, though. It'll be teeming with other potential customers. For anywhere from half a dozen to eighteen families live in those houses.

That in itself isn't so shocking. But what will surprise many people is that *Negroes* own them. Absentee Negroes.

A half-mile or so from this particular street begins a business section. Store after store is wedged into just a few short blocks, and rent is high. Why? Because the store-owners do a fantastic business. Their only problem is insurance. Sometimes they can't even get it, because the robbery rate is so high. So outside every store is a folding metal gate that costs more than anything inside.

There was a time when almost all of these stores were owned by whites. But that's past history. Now the majority are black-owned. And where there are white owners, they pay a hefty percentage to some Negro to run them and make sure a big profit is turned. He turns it, too, by selling everything from appliances and TV sets to clothes and jewelry and even food at twice what he should to people who don't know much better or don't care or would have trouble going elsewhere.

Some stores sell more in the back than out in the front. Bookies are everywhere. They're black. There are Negro dope pushers by the dozens, trying to start their own people on the road to hell as young as they can get them. Sometimes they'll give the kid the first two fixes for nothing to get him hooked. When the youngster—maybe he's eighteen, maybe he's twelve—needs more, he'll rob or murder to get the money. If the addict is a girl, she'll become a prostitute, though she might not have had her first period yet.

I can hear the blackthinkers screaming, "The white man built the houses and stores! The white man created the system and forced the black man to make a living by taking the bread out of his own brother's mouth!"

One look at the HELP WANTED section of any daily newpaper in just about any city in this country knocks that into a cocked hat. So does a look at all the *honest* Negro property owners and Negro entrepreneurs.

For the cold fact that almost every Negro, be he moderate or militant, wants to overlook—and that whites just don't know—is that *today the Negro is the greatest exploiter of the Negro.* It starts at the very bottom, with the portable hot-dog vendor who also sells heroin, and goes all the way up to the top, to many of the so-called "Negro leaders."

Take Adam Clayton Powell. Adam and I have broken bread together more than once, and I'm not sitting in judgment on him as a man. But as a representative of the Negro —that's something else. He doesn't walk among them, and he doesn't understand them anymore. Some of his constituents think he does because, like the blackthinkers, Adam knows how to exploit the feelings of certain of his people. But even when he's in Washington or New York within his plush suites, he's as far from the problems of Negroes—of *people*—as a leader can be.

Yet my point isn't to condemn Adam. The most important thing I'm trying to show isn't that the Negro is flawed. It's that he's *human*.

But why have I, who believe so strongly in showcasing the good, devoted page after page then to the bad, and to the "bad" that Negroes don't care to and whites won't dare to talk about?

To show that when it comes to prejudice, we're almost as guilty as the white.

To show that when it comes to copping out in the way we live as well as the way we think, we're just as guilty as the white.

To show that when it comes to the so-called exploitation of the Negro, the black man himself is first in line. The Negro is not the eternal masochist to the sadist white, and he shouldn't think of himself in this way. More than anyone else, he often has a vested interest in his brother's own poverty, ignorance and degradation. And so, in blackthink.

But just the fact that we are human is a key to this whole crisis, too. Human beings can be improved. I write this chapter to say to the black man what I've tried to say to myself for so many years. To paraphrase President Kennedy: Don't ask what the white man can do for you—don't even think of it—until you've first done every damned thing *you* can do for yourself.

10.

Open Letter
to a Young Negro

"Tell them how the good times between us were."
—Luz Long

"All black men are insane. . . . Almost any living thing
would quickly go mad under the unrelenting exposure to
the climate created and reserved for black men in a white
racist society. . . . I am secretly pleased about the riots.
Nothing would please the tortured man inside me more
than seeing bigger and better riots every day."

Those words were spoken by Bob Teague to his young
son in *Letters to a Black Boy*. He wrote these letters to
"alert" his son to "reality" so that the boy wouldn't "be
caught off guard—unprepared and undone."

Are his words true?

Does a black man have to be just about insane to exist in America?

Do all Negroes feel a deep twinge of pleasure every time we see a white man hurt and a part of white society destroyed?

Is reality something so stinking terrible that it'll grab your heart out of your chest with one hand and your manhood with the other if you don't meet it armed like a Nazi storm trooper?

Bob Teague is no "militant." He's a constructive, accomplished journalist with a wife and child. If he feels hate and fear, can *you* ever avoid feeling it?

Whether it's Uncle Tom or ranting rioter doing the talking today, you're told that you'll have to be afraid and angry. The only difference is that one tells you to hold it in and the other tells you to let it out. Life is going to be torture because you're a Negro, they all say. They only differ on whether you should grin and bear it or take it out on everyone else. But National Urban League official, Black Panther leader or any of the in-betweens all seem to agree on one thing today: "We must organize around our strongest bond—our blackness."

Is that really our strongest bond? Isn't there something deeper, richer, better in this world than the color of one's skin?

Let me tell you the answer to that. Let me prove it to you so strong and deep that you'll taste it for all the days to come. Let me throw my arm around your shoulder and walk you to where so much good is and where the only blackness worth fearing is the black they're trying to color your soul.

Even though you weren't born for ten, maybe twenty

years after, you've probably heard the story—the story of the 1936 Olympics and how I managed to come out with four gold medals. A lot of words have been written about those medals and about the one for the broad jump in particular. Because it was during that event that Hitler walked out on me and where, in anger, I supposedly fouled on my first two jumps against his prize athlete, Luz Long. The whole Olympics for me and, symbolically, for my country, seemed to rest on that third jump.

Yes, a lot of words have been written about that day and the days that followed. And they've almost been true, just as it's almost true that sometimes every black man weakens a little and does hate the white man, just as it's almost true that reality is tough at times and does make you want to weaken.

Yet, just like *those* "truths," what was written about me was only a half-truth without some other more important words. I want to say them to you now.

I *was* up against it, but long before I came to the broad jump. Negroes had gone to the Olympics before, and Negroes had won before. But so much more was expected of me. Because this was the time of the most intense conflict between dictatorship and freedom the world had ever known. Adolf Hitler was arming his country against the entire world, and almost everyone sensed it. It was ironic that these last Olympic Games before World War II was to split the earth were scheduled for Berlin, where he would be the host. From the beginning, Hilter had perverted the games into a test between two forms of government, just as he perverted almost everything else he touched.

Almost everything else.

The broad jump preliminaries came before the finals of

the other three events I was in—the hundred-meter and two-hundred-meter dashes and the relay. How I did in the broad jump would determine how I did in the entire Olympics. For here was where I held a world record that no one had ever approached before except one man: Luz Long, Hitler's best athlete.

Long, a tall, sandy-haired, perfectly built fellow (the ideal specimen of Hitler's "Aryan supremacy" idea), had been known to jump over twenty-six feet in preparing for the Games. No one knew for sure what he could really do because Hitler kept him under wraps. But stories had filtered out that he had gone as far as I had, farther than anyone else in the world. I was used to hearing rumors like that and tried not to think too much about it. Yet the first time I laid eyes on Long, I sensed that the stories hadn't been exaggerated. After he took his first jump, I knew they hadn't. This man was something. I'd have to set an Olympic record and by no small margin to beat him.

It would be tough. August in Berlin was muggier than May in Ann Arbor or Columbus. Yet the air was cool, and it was hard getting warmed up. The ground on the runway to the broad jump pit wasn't the same consistency as that at home. Long was used to it. I wasn't.

His first jump broke the Olympic record. In the trials!

Did it worry me a little? More than a little. He was on his home ground and didn't seem susceptible to the pressure. In fact, he'd already done one thing I always tried to do in every jumping event and race I ran: discourage the competition by getting off to a better start.

Well, there was only one way to get back the psychological advantage. Right off the bat I'd have to make a better jump than he did. I didn't want to do it that way—

it wasn't wise to use up your energy in preliminaries. Long could afford to showboat in the trials. This was his only event, the one he'd been groomed for under Hitler for years. I had to run three races besides, more than any other athlete on either team.

But I felt I had to make a showing right then. I measured off my steps from the takeoff board and got ready. Suddenly an American newspaperman came up to me. "Is it true, Jesse?" he said.

"Is what true?" I answered.

"That Hitler walked out on you? That he wouldn't watch you jump?"

I looked over at where the German ruler had been sitting. No one was in his box. A minute ago he had been there. I could add two and two. Besides, he'd already snubbed me once by refusing the Olympic Committee's request to have me sit in that box.

This was too much. I was mad, hate-mad, and it made me feel wild. I was going to show him. He'd hear about this jump, even if he wouldn't see it!

I felt the energy surging into my legs and tingling in the muscles of my stomach as it never had before. I began my run, first almost in slow motion, then picking up speed, and finally faster and faster until I was moving almost as fast as I did during the hundred-yard dash. Suddenly the takeoff board was in front of me. I hit it, went up, up high— so high I knew I was outdoing Long and every man who ever jumped.

But they didn't measure it. I heard the referee shout "Foul!" in my ears before I even came down. I had run too fast, been concentrating too much on a record and not enough on form. I'd gone half a foot over the takeoff board.

All the newspaper stories and books I've ever seen about that Olympic broad jump had me fouling on the next of my three tries, because the writers felt that made the story more dramatic. The truth is I didn't foul at all on my second jump.

I played it safe. Too safe. I was making absolutely sure I didn't foul. All right, I said to myself. Long had won his point. But who would remember the preliminaries tomorrow? It was the finals that counted. I had to make sure I got into those finals. I wasn't going to let him psyche me out of it. I wasn't going to let Hitler anger me into throwing away what I'd worked ten years for.

So I ran slower, didn't try to get up as high during my jump. Hell, I said to myself, if I can do twenty-six feet trying my best, I sure ought to be able to do a foot less without much effort. That would be enough to qualify for the finals, and there I'd have three fresh jumps again. That's where I'd take apart Luz Long.

It's funny how sometimes you can forget the most important things. I forgot that I wasn't the kind of guy who could ever go halfway at anything. More than that, no sprinter or jumper can really take just a little bit off the top. It's like taking a little bit off when you're working a mathematical equation or flying an airplane through a storm. You need the total concentration and total effort from beginning to end. One mistake and you're dead. More than that, my whole style was geared to giving everything I had, to using all my speed and energy every second of what I was doing. Once or twice I'd tried a distance race just for kicks. I was miserable at it. If I couldn't go all out all the time, I was no good.

So my second jump was no good.

I didn't foul. But I didn't go far enough to qualify, either. It wasn't just Long and Owens in the event anymore. There were dozens of other participants from other countries, and a bunch of them—too many—were now ahead of me.

I had one jump left.

It wasn't enough.

I looked around nervously, panic creeping into every cell of my body. On my right was Hitler's box. Empty. His way of saying I was a member of an inferior race who would give an inferior performance. In back of that box was a stadium containing more than a hundred thousand people, almost all Germans, all wanting to see me fail. On my right was the broad jump official. Was he fair? Yeah. But a Nazi. If it came to a close call, a hairline win-or-lose decision, deep down didn't he, too, want to see me lose? Worst of all, a few feet away was Luz Long, laughing with a German friend of his, unconcerned, confident, *Aryan*.

They were against me. Every one of them. I was back in Oakville again. I was a nigger.

Did I find some hidden resource deep within me, rise to the occasion and qualify for the finals—as every account of those Olympics says?

The hell I did.

I found a hidden resource, but it wasn't inside of me. It was in the most unlikely and revealing place possible.

Time was growing short. One by one the other jumpers had been called and taken their turns. What must have been twenty minutes or half an hour suddenly seemed like only seconds. I was going to be called next. I wasn't ready. I wanted to shout it—*I wasn't ready!*

Then the panic was total. I had to walk in a little circle to keep my legs from shaking, hold my jaw closed tight to stop my teeth from chattering. I didn't know what to do. I was lost, with no Charles Riley to turn to. If I gave it everything I had, I'd foul again. If I played it safe, I wouldn't go far enough to qualify. *And this is what it all comes down to,* I thought to myself. *Ten years and 4,500 miles to make a nigger of myself and not even reach the finals!*

And then I couldn't even think anymore. I started to feel faint, began to gasp for breath. Instinctively, I turned away from everyone so they couldn't see me. But I couldn't help hearing them. The thousands of different noises of the stadium congealed into one droning hum—*ch-ch-ch-ch ch-ch-ch-ch,* louder and louder in my ears. It was as though they were all chanting it. Hatefully, gleefully. *Ch-ch-ch-ch. Ch-ch-ch-ch. CH-CH-CH-CH.*

Suddenly I felt a firm hand on my arm. I turned and looked into the sky-blue eyes of my worst enemy.

"Hello, Jesse Owens," he said. "I am Luz Long."

I nodded. I couldn't speak.

"Look," he said. "There is no time to waste with manners. What has taken your goat?"

I had to smile a little in spite of myself—hearing his mixed-up American idiom.

"Aww, nothing," I said. "You know how it is."

He was silent for a few seconds. "Yes," he said finally, "I know how it is. But I also know you are a better jumper than this. Now, *what has taken your goat?*"

I laughed out loud this time. But I couldn't tell him, him above all. I glanced over at the broad jump pit. I was about to be called.

Luz didn't waste words, even if he wasn't sure of which ones to use.

"Is it what Reichskenzler Hitler did?" he asked.

I was thunderstruck that he'd say it. "I—" I started to answer. But I didn't know what to say.

"I see," he said, "Look, we talk about that later. Now you must jump. And you must qualify."

"But how?" I shot back.

"I have thought," he said. "You are like I am. You must do it one hundred percent. Correct?" I nodded. "Yet you must be sure not to foul." I nodded again, this time in frustration. And as I did, I heard the loudspeaker call my name.

Luz talked quickly. "Then you do both things, Jesse. You remeasure your steps. You take off six inches behind the foul board. You jump as hard as you can. But you need not fear to foul."

All at one the panic emptied out of me like a cloudburst. *Of course!*

I jogged over to the runway. I remeasured my steps again. Then I put a towel parallel to the place half a foot before the takeoff board from where I wanted to jump.

I walked back to the starting spot. I began my run, hit the place beside the towel, shot up into the air like a bird and qualified by more than a foot.

The next day I went into the finals of the broad jump and waged the most intense competition of my life with Luz Long. He broke his own personal record and the Olympic record, too, and then I—thanks to him—literally flew to top that. Hours before I had won the hundred meters in 10.3, and then afterward the 200 meters in 20.7 and helped our team to another gold medal and record in the relay.

During the evenings that framed those days, I would sit with Luz in his space or mine in the Olympic village, and we would form an even more intense friendship. We were sometimes as different inside as we looked on the outside. But the things that were the *same* were much more important to us.

Luz had a wife and a young child, too. His was a son. We talked about everything from athletics to art, but mostly we talked about the future. He didn't say it in so many words, but he seemed to know that war was coming and he would have to be in it. I didn't know then whether the United States would be involved, but I did realize that this earth was getting to be a precarious place for a young man trying to make his way. And, like me, even if war didn't come, Luz wasn't quite sure how he would make the transformation from athletics to life once the Olympics were over.

We talked, of course, about Hitler and what he was doing. Luz was torn between two feelings. He didn't believe in Aryan supremacy any more than he believed the moon was made of German cheese, and he was disturbed at the direction in which Hitler was going. Yet he loved his country and felt a loyalty to fight for it if it came to that, if only for the sake of his wife and son. I couldn't understand how he could go along with Hitler under any circumstances, though, and I told him so.

He wasn't angry when I said it. He just held out his hands and nodded. He didn't explain because he didn't understand completely himself, just as I couldn't explain to him how the United States tolerated the race situation. So we sat talking about these things, some nights later than two Olympic performers should have. We didn't come up with any final answers then, only with a unique friendship. For we were simply two uncertain young men in an uncertain world. One day we would learn the truth, but in the meantime, we would make some mistakes. Luz's mistake would cost him too much.

Yet we didn't make the mistake of not seeing past each other's skin color to what was within. If we couldn't apply that principle to things on a world scale, we still could live it fully in our own way in the few days we had together, the only days together we would ever have.

We made them count. We crammed as much understanding and fun as we could into every hour. We didn't even stop when we got out on the track. Luz was at my side cheering me on for every event, except the broad jump, of course. There he tried to beat me for all he was worth, but nature had put just a little more spring into my body and I went a handful of inches farther.

After he failed in his last attempt to beat me, he leaped out of the pit and raced to my side. To congratulate me. Then he walked toward the stands pulling me with him while Hitler was glaring, held up my hand and shouted to the gigantic crowd, "Jesse Owens! Jesse Owens!"

The stadium picked it up. "Jesse Owens!" they responded—though it sounded more like *Jaz-eee-ooh-wenz*. Each time I went for a gold medal and a record in the next three days, the crowd would greet me with "*Jaz-eee-ooh-wenz! Jaz-eee-ooh-wenz!*"

I'd had people cheering me before, but never like this. Many of those men would end up killing my countrymen, and mine theirs, but the truth was that they didn't want to, and would only do it because they "had" to. Thanks to Luz, I learned that the false leaders and sick movements of this earth must be stopped in the beginning, for they turn humanity against itself.

Luz and I vowed to write each other after the Games, and we did. For three years we corresponded regularly, though the letters weren't always as happy as our talks at the Olympics had been. Times were hard for me and harder for Luz. He had had to go into the German army, away from his wife and son. His letters began to bear strange postmarks. Each letter expressed more and more doubt about what he was doing. But he felt he had no other choice. He was afraid for his family if he left the army. And how could they leave Germany? It was Luz's world, just as the South had been the only world for so many Negroes.

The last letter I got from him was in 1939. "Things become more difficult," he said, "and I am afraid, Jesse. Not just the thought of dying. It is that I may die for the wrong thing. But whatever might become of me, I hope only that my wife and son will stay alive. I am asking you who are my only friend outside of Germany, to someday visit them if you are able, to tell them about why I had to do this, and how the good times between us were. Luz."

I answered right away, but my letter came back. So did the next, and the one after. I inquired about Luz through a dozen channels. Nothing. A war was on. Finally, when it was over, I was able to get in touch with Luz's wife and find out what had happened to him. He was buried somewhere in the African desert.

Luz Long had been my competition in the Olympics. He was a white man—a Nazi white man who fought to destroy my country.

I loved Luz Long, as much as my own brothers. I still love Luz Long.

I went back to Berlin a few years ago and met his son,

another fine young man. And I told Karl about his father. I told him that, though fate may have thrown us against one another, Luz rose above it, rose so high that I was left with not only four gold medals I would never have had, but with the priceless knowledge that the only bond worth anything between human beings is their humanness.

Today there are times when that bond doesn't seem to exist. I know. I felt the same way before my third jump at the 1936 Olympics, as well as a thousand other times. There've been many moments when I did feel like hating the white man, all white men, felt like giving in to fearful reality once and for all.

But I've learned those moments aren't the real me. And what's true of me is true of most men I've met. My favorite speech in a movie is the scene in *High Noon* when Gary Cooper, alone and hunted by the four sadistic killers, momentarily weakens and saddles a horse to get out of town. Like everyone else, his deputy wants him to do it and helps him. But Cooper finally won't get up on the horse.

"Go on!" his deputy shouts. "Do it!"

"I can't do it," Cooper says.

"You were going to a minute ago!"

"I was tired," Cooper tells him. "A man thinks a lotta things when he's tired. But I *can't do it.*"

We all get tired. But know yourself, know your humanness, and you'll know why you can never finally throw in with the bigotry of blackthink. You must not be a Negro. You must be a human being first and last, if not always.

Reach back, Harry Edwards. Reach back inside yourself and grapple for that extra ounce of guts, that last cell of manhood even you didn't know you had, that something that let you stand the pain and beat the ghetto and go on to break the records. Use it now to be totally honest with yourself.

For when the chips are really down, you can either put your skin first or you can go with what's inside it.

Sure, there'll be times when others try to keep you from being human. But remember that prejudice isn't new. It goes way back, just as slavery goes way back, to before there ever was an America. Men have always had to meet insanity without losing their own minds.

That doesn't mean you should stand still for bigotry. Fight it. Fight it for all you're worth. But fight your *own* prejudice, too. Don't expect perfection in your white brother until there's not an ounce of blackthink left in you. And remember that the hardest thing for all of us isn't to fight, but to stop and think. *Black, think* . . . is the opposite of . . . *blackthink.*

I'm not going to play any Establishment games with you. My way isn't its own reward. Self-knowledge, getting rid of the bitterness, a better life are the rewards.

So be a new kind of "militant," an *immoderate moderate,* one hundred percent involved, but as a man, not a six-foot hunk of brown wrapping paper, be an extremist when it comes to your ideals, a moderate when it comes to the raising of your fist.

Live every day deep and strong. Don't pass up *your* Olympics and *your* Luz Long. Don't let the blackthinkers sell you out for a masquerade rumble where the real you can never take off the mask.

You see, black *isn't* beautiful.

White isn't beautiful.

Skin-deep is *never* beautiful.

11.

Open Letter
to All Whites

During the last Olympics, a number of Negro athletes became close with white fellows on the team. This was the
rule, by the way, not the exception. But a certain pair in
particular became especially good buddies and reminded
me some of the friendship I had had with Luz Long in the
Berlin Olympics. They cheered each other on during the
competition, ate together off the field and just did a lot of
walking and talking—finding out how much they had in
common.

When it came time to go home, the white fellow asked
his Negro pal to come to his house and stay for a week. "I
know Dad would love to have you," he added.

The Negro nodded quietly. "But would he give me a job?" he said sarcastically.

The white athlete was shocked. But then he thought it over and saw the point. He still asked his buddy to come to the house, but only after he'd phoned his father from Mexico City and secured a job interview for the friend. As it turned out, the man did give his son's pal a job. But not because the Negro was a friend. Because he was competent and eager to work. In less than two years, the young man has been promoted twice and is making $16,000 annually. He's married now and lives in a suburb near the business with his wife and baby. He sees his white benefactor socially every two or three months, but neither the father nor the son are really benefactors, because the Negro junior exec is doing just as much for them as they are for him. He's helping to make a business grow.

Yet it never would've happened if the Negro hadn't come out and asked for that job. His white brother would've had him out to the house for a week, would have had him waited on hand and foot and the father *would* have loved having him there.

But they never would have dreamed of offering work to him. And work is the most important thing, more important even than friendship.

It was for me in 1936, too. I told you how I came home from the Olympics to the irony of parades and poverty. But why I came home when I did is part of that story too.

After my last event in the Olympics, I wanted to pack up and go home. I was tired, bone tired. For the first time I knew how my father must have felt working the fields in Oakville sixteen hours a day. The Olympic Games hadn't been just fun and games. I'd been working as hard as I could physically to prepare for them for over a year, and the few days in which I competed in more than a dozen trials and finals were the straw that broke the camel's back.

Even more, there was the emotional factor. All the fears and hopes that had been bottled up in me since I was a kid had been waiting for this one chance. Then, to top it off I'd had the scene with Hitler and the near-disaster in the broad jump. Luz Long had saved me from that, but the unbelievable ups and downs of the week were just too much. I was all used up. I wanted to go home.

The night after the relay, I went back to my room and threw myself on the cot. Luz had had some official task to perform that evening, so I just lay there and tried to make up for lost rest.

But I was too tired to sleep. I couldn't relax. I watched the moon move in the sky from east to west until finally it was a hazy part of a circle against the dawn.

I got up and tried to have a good breakfast. Just lying there must have done me some good, I figured. It didn't matter that much anyway. I was going home that day and was glad of it. There had been too much time away from Ruth and the family, too much time away from my real life. Because from almost the moment the relay was over, I'd started thinking about my future.

Even though this was all I'd done for a dozen years and though I'd gotten as good as any man in the world at it, I knew that running and jumping no longer held a permanent place in my life. It wasn't pleasant seeing that, but better to face it then than later, I decided. Best to get home, pitch in and start the business of life. The hardest part was

leaving Luz. We saw each other the day of the closing cere-
monies and tried to make what we had to say last for a long
time.

Then he was gone. I had made an extraordinary friend,
but I still had to live my own life. I'd begun packing when
Ralph Metcalfe rushed up to me. Ralph was a fellow who
always kept his cool, so I was surprised to see him unstrung.

"Forget the packing, Jesse," he said. "Just grab your
spikes and togs and let's get out of here. We've got a train
to catch!"

The Amateur Athletic Union had scheduled another
meet for some of the members of the American Olympic
squad. It was probably the first of many, Ralph huffed and
puffed to me as we literally did run to catch the train. I
hurriedly scrawled Dave Albritton a note to bring the rest
of my stuff with him. I didn't have time to send a telegram
to Ruth or to my mother, though I wouldn't have been able
to even if there'd been ten minutes extra. I was broke.

I'd boarded the ship for Europe with seven dollars and
forty cents in my pocket. That pocket was in my only suit, a
blue striped one I'd had for four years. It was small on me.
Now I was boarding a train, the suit rumpled, not a penny
to my name, fifteen pounds underweight from two weeks of
the most rugged competition possible and so tired I felt
sick to my stomach.

I lost at Cologne, Germany. That made me truly sick,
mentally as well as physically. I had tarnished my Olympic
performances, the medals I'd won and the friendship with
Luz, who helped me gain those medals. It really stung deep,
and the hurt didn't leave as we traveled on to the next place
and the next. The day came real soon when I knew I
couldn't let it happen anymore.

I was walking off the track with Ralph when Larry Snyder crossed over to us. There was a strange look on his face. "Keep washing your sweat clothes, guys," he said. "I just got a telegram. The AAU wants you to run in Sweden tomorrow."

I didn't say anything for a full minute. If there'd been an AAU official there, I might have hit him. The AAU simply didn't understand. Just as they so often don't understand today. They'd never thought of finding me a job somewhere for when I got home and *then* asking me to run "one more time" and one more time after that. They'd never dreamed of trying to break a Negro into professional baseball or football. I would have been the perfect guinea pig with my "world's fastest human" reputation.

No, they thought of me as their performing monkey, a running machine that never broke down and that would do some p-r work for America while mainly doing a lot more good for the old AAU.

Well, the monkey wasn't going to perform anymore. He'd lost at Cologne, and he wasn't going to make a habit of it at Stockholm and at the next place after that and the next and the next.

Not that it was the losing that hurt most. It was what Pierre de Coubertin, the founder of the modern Olympics had said: "The purpose is not winning, but fighting well." I didn't have any more of that kind of fight left in me. Ruth was waiting. Little Gloria was waiting. My mother and father and college were waiting. My *responsibilities*.

"Can I borrow a little from you till we get home, Larry?" I asked.

"Sure," he said right away, fishing into his pocket and bringing out whatever money he had on him.

I took what I needed, thanked him and said what I was going to do with it. Then I went and did it—sent a telegram to the AAU. It said:

> Sick and underweight. Cannot compete in Stockholm. Family waiting for me. Going home. Jesse Owens.

Two hours later I got a telegram back from them. It notified me that I was suspended from the Amateur Athletic Union and was never again to compete as an amateur athlete for the United States.

That tore it. If I'd had any slight ideas left of doing something in sports, maybe going for a final record in my last year at Ohio State, they were dead. If I'd had any hope even of running a few exhibitions at home to set myself up for an outside job in sports, it was gone. To tell the truth, I didn't care that much right then. I just wanted to get one good night's sleep.

But I cared later. Not only because the AAU had shut me out without ever really letting me in, but because the world was doing the same thing. Jesus, how I needed a job once I got back home.

Many Negroes are in the same boat today in a way. I know I've said there's opportunity all around us so thick you can cut it and that the want ads of the paper are a daily testimonial to the fact that anyone who wants work can find it.

But there are two hitches. First, a Negro doesn't want just any job. Like a white man, he wants the right job. Second, the right job more and more in our society is the one that requires training. There are fewer and fewer ads for laborers and more and more for computer specialists. And it applies to more than computers, too. Not long ago, for instance, *TV Guide* ran an article on the staggering number of jobs for which no training was needed open to Negroes in television—jobs that weren't even being applied for. Or take a look at Dave Albritton. Last year he finally opened a bank in Ohio. It took him three years from the time he'd gotten the money. Because he didn't have the Negroes to work in it.

This happens partly because so many Negroes have been brainwashed by blackthink. But it also happens because so many blacks aren't trained to do the jobs available. In a sense most whites are trained for generations to fit into many of the roles society offers. To Negroes, this is something new. Though I consider it a really incomparable achievement that my great-grandfather survived slavery and that my father left Oakville for the North, only a handful of Negroes are "third-generation achievers" in the terms of our modern world.

Whites can help remedy this, help fast and sure and do themselves some good at the same time simply by supplying training. Training, training, training—that's what it's all about in our economic society today. The white conservatives with their grandiose ideas of "black capitalism" don't realize that a man without the means to gain capital is never going to be a capitalist. The white liberals with their bleeding hearts and paternalistic handouts don't see that socialism and self-reliance can never make it together.

I know one white man who must spend forty hours a week in "philanthropic" work. He makes speeches. He takes food baskets to the ghetto. He attends conferences on discrimination. Forty hours a week he pours water through a sieve. What he should be doing all those hours is not running away from the stuff of his life—the business he built that employs more than a thousand people (of which only a handful are Negroes)—but *be there,* instituting training programs so that he won't fail in finding Negroes for the right jobs next year and the year after and five years from now.

Give jobs before friendship. Give speeches only if you've provided training to make the message of those speeches work.

But at the same time don't throw in with the black-thinking "we don't need whites for our friends" party line. Whites *can* help the race crisis on a level ultimately as important as the economic one.

But not the way they've been doing it.

You probably noticed another by-line on this book in addition to mine. It's the name of the writer I've worked with for over ten years, the fellow who helps make my thoughts into words. He's often pretty militant, but I've been able to work with him for that long a time and forge a closer friendship year after year partly because he's more free of prejudice than just about any white man I've ever known.

But he's still bigoted as hell sometimes.

And he knows it.

A few weeks before I completed this book, Paul told me of an experience he had. He lives in a suburb of Chicago where there are an increasing number, yet still only a small percentage, of Negroes. One day his eight-year-old son forgot to take lunch along to school and Paul drove over to drop it off.

He didn't know where the boy would be at that hour, so he waited in the principal's office while they called his son from his classroom. "While I was waiting," Paul told me, "one class lined up outside for some kind of assembly. There were about twenty of them. My eyes ran over them, and then stopped on a little Negro girl. She was cute as a button, was my first thought," he told me. "But no, that wasn't my first thought, I admitted to myself. Let's face it. There were other cute kids there. My first thought was that *she was a Negro.* I averted my eyes right away, but it was too late. Most of the kids had been looking into the principal's glassed office, and she'd seen me stare at her for that briefest of instants. I wondered how many other times in her short life she had had white eyes do this to her and how many more times she'd have to go through it. And even if she hadn't seen me, Jesse, *I* saw me. I saw bigotry inside myself, way inside where no one-day surgery will cut it out."

What happened to that little girl in that split second is what happens to Negroes almost every hour of every day for their entire lives. You can learn to understand and overcome it, but that doesn't make it go down any better. And even the most "unprejudiced" whites are guilty. That almost automatic reaction, that reaction which says "they are different," never escapes a Negro's notice. If he's a man about things, he won't hate you for it. But he won't fool himself, either. For those little glances and slips in conversation always tell him one thing: he's still looking in from the outside in the most important way of all.

As a human being.

What can *you* do about it?

You can *change,* Whitey.

You can try like hell to retrain and rethink your everyday reactions by digging out your deepest thoughts and habits. You can take a few of those precious minutes that you spend watching the baseball game or the soap operas on TV, or an hour from the job that's getting you ahead in the world, or even a night that you would've spent at some anti-poverty conference and just do some hard thinking. Because, let's not kid ourselves, thinking is the hardest thing to do.

Don't believe that because you give time and money to civil rights you've really given what counts most. Don't believe that because one or two or even "some" of your best friends are Negroes, you're free of bigotry. Don't believe that because your mind accepts liberty and justice for all, your guts are one hundred percent sold on it.

Frankly, I don't know that any Negro old enough to read this will ever live in a world without the gut reactions of prejudice staring him in the face. I don't know that any white reading this, even if he starts now to try and free himself of his bigotry, will ever be able to succeed more than a small percentage of the time.

But I do know that those few successes will count for a lot.

And the failures will be a *different kind* of failure.

The Negro isn't asking you to undo *your* centuries of hell all at once—the hell that was stamped onto *your* innocent mind when you were told whites were better. All he's asking, and what he deserves, is for you to fight that hell.

In another suburb of Chicago there is a row of twelve town houses. In one lives a twenty-eight-year-old white man with a wife and a young son. John is average height, has an average job and looks pretty much like an average guy. But he's not.

Two houses down from him live a fifty-five-year-old Negro construction foreman and his wife. Their children are grown, so they recently bought a dog—a toy poodle—for companionship. The poodle and its owner make an odd sight. Nate is six feet four inches tall, with hands like hams.

He's a rather finely drawn fellow, though, who might have fit into a university professor's chair if he'd had the education. As it is, he has bookcases lining walls of three of his six rooms and, yes, he's "read all those books."

Nate and his wife are the only Negroes in the twelve town houses, and they nod to their neighbors but never try to make friends. Nate is kind of a lonely man, but much, much prouder than he is lonely.

John got a dog for his boy, a big Labrador, and one day was walking it where Nate had his poodle.

"How are you?" John said.

"Good, and you?" Nate answered a little stiffly.

They just led their dogs around for a minute without being able to think of anything else to say. Then John asked Nate something about toy poodles—were they easy to train?

Nate began talking. John asked another question. It was good talk and the right questions, because here was a subject they were both avidly interested in, here were two men meeting as real human beings with a common interest, not a couple of cardboard imitations "confronting" one another.

"And we haven't had any trouble with him on the rug," Nate was going on. "I think three weeks ago, on a Tuesday it was, was the last time he—he made—made—"

Suddenly Nate stopped. All the old inhibitions rose up. He was talking to a white man again, talking to a man who might think the less of him, whom he might offend if he said one wrong word.

"—doo-doo," the six-foot-four-inch construction foreman finished.

John caught the meaning of the moment immediately and had the guts to do something about it before it passed out of sight and their communication with it. He wasn't going to allow that invisible but impenetrable wall to stay there.

"*Doo-doo?*" he said. "You mean *shit,* don't you?"

Nate laughed loud and rich in his deep chest. Tears came to eyes he laughed so loud. John was laughing with him. "That's just what I meant," Nate said, smiling. "That's *exactly* what I meant!"

There's no white man or woman in this world who can't do what John did.

And what he accomplished that day—without trying to "accomplish" anything but only wanting to be human—is more important than who he votes for in the next election or how much money he contributes to civil rights causes. For one stare can undo a hundred laws. One hand held out in sincere humanity can make a lot of laws unnecessary.

Only when you're totally committed to fighting white-think can you battle blackthink. But don't make the mistake of feeling then that blackthink is any less insidious than the white brand of bigotry. If Rap Brown and Harry Edwards were the only kind of blackthinkers, the war against them would already be won. The blackthinkers who really count are much more difficult to spot and to fight. They're not just black militants who actually feel that their kinky hair makes them superior to whites just as Hitler's Aryans used to feel superior because of their wavy blond hair. Nor are they only white women hung up on the Negro's supposed sex prowess. They're people like me—or *you.*

Last winter, for example, several Negro teen-age boys from Louisville's poorer sections got together and decided to sell magazine subscriptions for money. Only they decided to sell these subscriptions in the plushest white residential neighborhoods. It cost them more money for transportation that way, but the results justified it. They set records. Hardly a house refused them.

Enterprising of the Negroes? Generous of the whites?

Not by a long shot. Each of those boys was a black-thinker, one of the worst kind, and in almost every case so were the whites.

It was out of fear that the whites bought subscriptions to magazines they didn't want. They were paying off. Here was a tall Negro boy walking up their manicured lawn. Fear. But wait—he only wants me to spend eight dollars on *Harper's*. What a small price to pay, eh? Give in, pay it. Be thankful he's here to sell subscriptions and not to set fire to the house. Pay the blackmail.

And the Negroes? They knew it. That's why they picked the neighborhoods they did. They knew they had blackthink going for them, that the threat of riot was right underneath the polite smile and list of publications. But they don't want to riot. You could get hurt. They don't want to waste time demonstrating. They want to make money, or go to college, maybe just buy a shiny car. And they want to do it by climbing on someone's back. They want to stay right smack in the middle of the Establishment by using the threat of militancy.

Giving in to that kind of blackthink even at its most subtle is no different from giving in to whitethink. Columbia University's Negro Professor Charles Hamilton calls this the "new kind of paternalism," a kind that will do just as much harm as the old one.

Yet at the same time there are many demands being made by blacks today that are more than justified, demands

that should have been met centuries ago, because they are
rights. The water muddies when you mix a good cause with
a not-so-good person.

Karen is a wealthy liberal. Though aging some, she's
still more than attractive and seems a good ad for all the
causes she marches in. Karen demonstrates every chance she
gets and has been doing it since her early twenties.

Her first marriage failed after six years. Her second
seemed better but broke up when she became involved in
an affair with a Negro. She married again in her middle
thirties, but that marriage has ended in a separation.

Two children came out of the marriages. Karen brings
them up with all the latest methods, but every once in a while
she hauls off and whips them unmercifully. They are nine
and four, and during the Democratic Convention, she left
them alone all night while she reveled in the violence down-
town.

I know the Negro with whom she had the affair that
ended her second marriage. Once, after he'd broken up with
her, he came to me for advice on a business matter. He got
to talking, and before I knew it he was telling me about it.
"She's so bright and such a beauty," he said. "But she's
sick inside, Jesse. I hated to, but I finally had to end it."

"How is she sick?" I asked.

He hesitated for a moment. "She's one of *those* women,"
he said. "She . . . needs pain. She always wanted me to hit
her before I . . . made love to her."

The story is secondhand, but it fits too well. It fits for
many a blackthinker, both white and Negro. For if revenge
is what makes militants tick, then guilt and the need for
punishment—and the violence that is always at the heart of
punishment—is the motivation of many nonmilitant whites

and Negroes. In some cases, it can even kick them over into extremism. If they defensively deny the guilt they feel, they'll become militant *right* wingers instead of left. But the violence is always there. And blacks who are really dedicated hate this kind of blackthinker worse than any other.

The sad thing is that most of the guilt isn't real. You don't inherit shame. And if you weren't really sharply aware until now of what the Negro has gone through, you can't indict yourself for life because of it. Even if for a long time you sensed that there was injustice all around you, even if you *were* guilty of turning away from it and insulating yourself against it, the answer isn't to wear a hair shirt for the rest of your life.

Hair shirts don't help us.

So what I'm really saying is to give yourself a chance. And give us a chance with it.

Maybe we *do* have rhythm. Maybe our sweat *does* have a different odor. Well, it's too bad you don't have rhythm. And your sweat smells different to us. Who in the hell cares? I don't. Because I know all the other things we have that matter so much more.

They're the same things *you* have. They're what being a human being is all about.

12.

We Shall Overcome
—If

"The great valley of the Umzimkulu is still in darkness, but the light will come there. Ndotsheni is still in darkness, but the light will come there also. For it is the dawn that has come, as it has come for a thousand centuries, never failing. But when that dawn will come, of our emancipation, from the fear of bondage and the bondage of fear, why, that is a secret."
— Alan Paton in *Cry, The Beloved Country*

What color is Utopia?

I know—how can a Negro ever use the word Utopia? But even with the violence that is exploding around us, even though it's taken hundreds of years to produce the mess we got ourselves into and is going to take a hell of a long time to get completely out, I think there are signs that someday a realistic kind of "Utopia" actually will come about.

That the young are so serious about things—unfortunately sometimes even to the point of violence—is one hopeful sign. I hate, really hate, their ravaging universities and clubbing professors, but I also think the deeper meaning of everything from hippie to yippie is that some things much more basic than college curriculums have to be changed in this country. The days of Establishment for Establishment's sake are over. Today's youth aren't going to live their lives by any races that were run in 1936.

At the same time, though, the mature humor mushrooming up today is just as important a sign of progress to me as the intense seriousness. Throughout this book I've often made a point by telling a humorous story. It's no accident. Negro-white humor is turning into a dialogue all its own, maybe a more meaningful one than any other, and it tells you a lot about what the future holds. When Slappy White says he marched with Dick Gregory in one-hundred-degree temperature, for instance, and decided he'd rather be in the back of an air-conditioned bus, he isn't throwing out his ideals or throwing in with the whitethinkers. He's expressing a deep truth felt by the vast majority of Negroes and whites—that any "principle" that doesn't do you any good in practice is no damn good.

The white man hears this humor. He laughs. But how often does he get the message?

Well, I'll tell you something: I don't even think most Negroes have been getting the message.

That was my first purpose in writing *Blackthink*—not only to help the white man know the Negro but, equally as important, to help the Negro to know himself.

There are no fancy lists of A, B, C, sub 1, sub 2, sub 3 here. Yet I hope there are no empty platitudes, either. At least, I tried to fill the platitudes with the stuff of my experience, the lesson of my own life. It's a life that parallels the race crisis, because I've been there—I *started there* and *went back*—both as man and Negro. The story of Jesse Owens is no Horatio Alger yarn. It's the black's story, the story of a man whose past chained him. It took me half a century to exist on what I could do, not what I'd done. The Negro has taken many centuries to begin to do what he can do and not revolve around only what was done to him.

I'm not saying every new day isn't a learning experience for me. And I'm not telling you I don't miss more than I catch some of those days. Things keep changing, so fast, and you have to somehow change with them. When I went back to Berlin to meet Luz's son Karl I took a look at the stone where my name had been etched. The words *Jesse Owens* were still there. But there were bullet holes beside them.

Still, no matter how much you change or grow, I think some things inside you—just like inside a country—must stay the same. If I still have a lot to learn in this world, none of if will be from bigots. America has nothing to learn from them, either.

This was my second purpose in writing this book—to drive the first real nail in the coffin of blackthink. Oh, most people are against it, but they're unknowingly against blackthink on blackthink's terms, or on the old Establishment terms. For what blackthink is threatening to do, even to those who disagree with it, is to further alienate the Negro from the world in which he lives. I wanted, in an emotional way before any other, to help bring my people back to the human family—back to my *other* people, if you please.

It's a lot bigger job, I know, than breaking records in the hundred-yard dash. But it can be done. It's *being* done. Every day people in this world are communicating more and more, not as white and Negro, not as employer and employee, but as *human being* and *human being.*

Yet before a man can have a dialogue with anybody else, he has to have a dialogue with himself. You have to tell it like it is to your own soul before you can ever make sense to anyone else's.

I'll never forget the story a young ghetto preacher told on himself to me a few months ago. He was very progressive, even though almost every one of his parishioners was bone poor. He was doing what he could for them, but above all wanted to buy a set of books for the Sunday school library so the youngsters could be educated. This took money, and his congregation simply didn't have any. But he felt that if he could only be eloquent enough, if he could only get the message across just once of how important it was for them to buy these books, they'd each give what little they had and it would somehow add up to just enough.

He worked for weeks on his speech, making every word exactly what it should be, each thought what it had to be. Then, when the sermon was polished like a jewel, he took half the savings he and his wife had put together, over a hundred dollars, and purchased a shiny twenty-dollar gold piece.

The day came, and he stepped before his congregation to speak. It was filled to capacity with his poverty-stricken parishioners, possibly because he had put up so many notices in the neighborhood, and he was in high spirits with the prospect of success. Somehow, a few pennies here, maybe a dollar there, and the library would become a reality. He spoke more eloquently that day than he ever had, ending with a passionate plea for the books.

Then he took the collection box and held the shining

gold piece above it, frankly telling his people what it represented to him and his family. Half their savings. And he
dropped it in.

The collection box went from person to person, row to
row to row and finally back to the front. The preacher shook
hands with the people as they filed out. When he was alone,
he opened it up.

Inside was one coin—his own gold piece.

He stood there silently for a long moment, fighting to
hold back the tears. Then, slowly, his expression changed.
Something like a smile touched his mouth.

"You know, baby," he whispered to himself, "it's too bad
you didn't put a lot more into that thing. 'Cause if you did,
you would've had a lot more to take out."